THE ILLITERATE DIGEST

THE ILLITERATE DIGEST
OFFICE
WILL ROGERS - PROP.
OUR POLICY IS "NOTHING IS NO GOOD!"
NATE Collier

THE ILLITERATE DIGEST

By WILL ROGERS

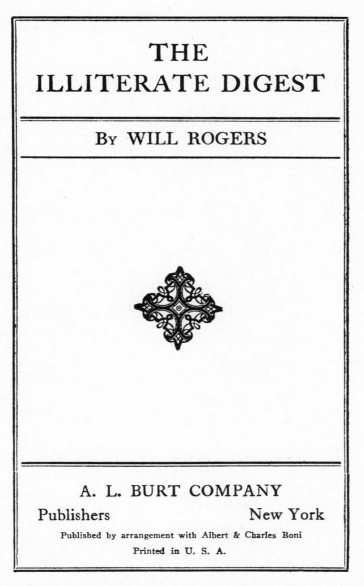

A. L. BURT COMPANY

Publishers New York

Published by arrangement with Albert & Charles Boni

Printed in U. S. A.

Republished by Gale Research Company, Book Tower, Detroit, 1974

This is a facsimile reprint of the 1924 edition published in New York by The A.L. Burt Company.

Library of Congress Cataloging in Publication Data

Rogers, Will, 1879-1935.
The illiterate digest.

Reprint of the 1924 ed.
I. Title.
PN6161.R66 1974 818'.5'207 77-145720
ISBN 0-8103-3975-7

TWO LETTERS AND A DEDICATION

Most Books have to have an Excuse by some one for the Author, but this is the only Book ever written that has to have an Alibi for the Title, too. About 4 years ago, out in California, I was writing sayings for the Screen and I called it the Illiterate Digest. Well one day up bobs the following letter from this N. Y. Lawyer. It and the answer are absolutely just as they were exchanged at that time.

WILLIAM BEVERLY WINSLOW
LAWYER

55 Liberty Street,
New York, N. Y.

Nov. 5th, 1920.

Will Rogers, Esq.,
c/o Goldwyn Studios,
Culver City, Calif.

Dear Sir:—

My client, the Funk & Wagnalls Company, publishers of the "Literary Digest" have requested me to write to you in regard to your use of the phrase, "The Illiterate Digest," as a title to a moving picture subject gotten up by you, the consequence of which may have escaped your consideration.

For more than two years past it (my client) has placed upon the moving picture screen a short reel subject carrying the title "Topics of the Day," selected from the Press of the World by "The Literary Digest." This subject has achieved a wide popularity both because of the character and renown of "The Literary Digest" and through the expenditure of much time, effort and money by its owners in presenting the subject to the public. "The Literary Digest" is a publication nearly thirty years old, and from a small beginning has become probably the most influential weekly publication in the world. Its name and the phrase "Topics of the Day" are fully covered by usage as trademarks as well as by registration as such in the United States Patent Office.

During several months past your "title," "The Illiterate Digest" has been repeatedly called to our attention and we are told that the prestige of "The Literary Digest" is being lowered by the subject matter of your film as well as by the title of your film because the public naturally confuse the two subjects. We are also told that exhibitors are being misled by the similarity of titles and that some of them install your subject in the expectation that they are securing "The Literary Digest Topics of the Day."

It seems to me self-evident that your title would scarcely have been thought of or adopted had it not been for our magazine and for our film. If this were not the case the title which you use would be without significance to the general public.

I have advised the publishers that they may proceed against you through the Federal Trade Commission in Washington calling upon you to there defend yourself against the charge of "unfair competition," because of your simulation of their title, or that they can proceed against you, the producers of your film, its distributors and exhibitors in court for an injunction restraining you from use of the title, "The Illiterate Digest."

Before, however, instituting any proceedings in either direction they have suggested that I write directly to you to see if your sense of fairness will not cause you to voluntarily withdraw the use of the objectionable title.

Unless I hear favorably from you on or before the first of December, I shall conclude that you are not willing to accede to this suggestion and will take such steps as I may deem advisable.

Yours truly,

WBW/als

(signed) William Beverly Winslow.

Los Angeles, Cal.,
Nov. 15, 1920.

MR WM BEVERLY WINSLOW,

Dear Sir,

Your letter in regard to my competition with the Literary Digest received and I never felt as swelled up in my life, And am glad you wrote directly to me instead of communicating with my Lawyers, As I have not yet reached that stage of prominence where I was commiting unlawful acts and requireing a Lawyer, Now if the Literary Digest feels that the competition is to keen for them—to show you my good sportsmanship I will withdraw, In fact I had already quit as the gentlemen who put it out were behind in their payments and my humor kinder waned, in fact after a few weeks of no payments I couldent think of a single joke. And now I want to inform you truly that this is the first that I knew my Title of the Illiterate Digest was an infringement on yours as they mean the direct opposite, If a magazine was published called Yes and another Bird put one out called No I suppose he would be infringeing. But you are a Lawyer and its your business to change the meaning of words, so I lose before I start,

Now I have not written for these people in months and they havent put any gags out unless it is some of the old ones still playing. If they are using gags that I wrote on topical things 6 months ago then I must admit that they would be in competition with the ones the Literary Digest Screen uses now. I will gladly furnish you with their address, in case you want to enter suit, And as I have no Lawyer you can take my case too and whatever we get out of them we will split at the usual Lawyer rates of 80-20, the client of course getting the 20,

Now you inform your Editors at once that their most dangerous rival has withdrawn, and that they can go ahead and resume publication, But you inform Your clients that if they ever take up Rope Throwing or chewing gum that I will consider it a direct infringement of my rights and will protect it with one of the best Kosher Lawyers in Oklahoma,

Your letter to me telling me I was in competition with the Digest would be just like Harding writing to Cox and telling him he took some of his votes,

So long Beverly if you ever come to California, come out to Beverly where I live and see me

Illiterately yours

WILL ROGERS.

When I sent him my answer I read it to some of the Movie Company I was working with at the time and they kept asking me afterwards if I had received an answer. I did not, and I just thought, oh well, there I go and waste a letter on some High

Brow Lawyer with no sense of humor. I was sore at myself for writing it. About 6 months later I came back to join the Follies and who should come to call on me but the nicest old Gentleman I had ever met, especially in the law profession. He was the one I had written the letter to, and he had had Photographic Copies made of my letter and had given them around to all his Lawyer friends.

So it is to him and his sense of humor, that I dedicate this Volume of deep thought. I might also state that the Literary Digest was broad-minded enough to realize that there was room for both, and I want to thank them for allowing me to announce my Illiteracy publicly.

CONTENTS

CONTENTS

* With apologies to Arthur Brisbane.

ILLUSTRATIONS

ILLUSTRATIONS

INTRODUCTION

This book should have been long before now on the Bookshelves of every reader of worth while Literature in the English speaking World, in addition to being well worn in our best reference Libraries, and should have been already translated into every known and unknown tongue. What you will immediately ask delayed such an important event? Well the principal reason is it had not been written, and the next is We had no introduction for it. You let a Book go out without an Alibi by some other writer, and it is practically a commercial suicide. When the Publishers were all clamoring for a Book from me, and were practically annihilating (Boy there is a word I never used before in my life and I hope it fits in, I read it in some War Novel) each other for the Publishing rights and assured profits, they of course felt that through my wide Literary acquaintance, gained during years of association at the Democratic National Convention, and the late World Series with some of the best contemporary Writers of modern times, I should through my Literary standing and personal friendship, allow some of them to have the honor of penning the introduction to this Time Table of National Catastrophes.

William Emporia Allen White was my first thought, on account of his having a middle name, which always sounds Literary, even if its owner is not. Then I had heard he himself had written a Book once, and by now should know what Introductions should not be. Then he went home and announced himself as a Candidate for Governor. So that eliminated him from my thoughts. To have a big broad-minded book have any narrow Political endorsement would mean certain calamity among people who think. To run for Governor is bad enough, But to run for Governor of Kansas and then write an Introduction of my worthy efforts, would simply make the book a laughing stock.

Then my thoughts turned to Arthur Brisbane, I don't know what I could have been eating that my thoughts should have done such a mental somersault. But I guess it was because I had known Arthur for years,—I knew him before William Randolph Hearst started working for him. I approached him on it, and he said, Sorry Will but what I write must point a moral, there must be a lesson in every paragraph; mine must not only be news but it must be instructive news. For instance, I read China will not go to war on rainy days. What does that bit of news mean to the individual that dont think? Nothing! What does it mean to me? It means that a Chinaman would rather get shot than wet. It points a moral to peace: Have all so-called civilized Nations stop wars on rainy days. Then hold all wars in Portland, Oregon where it rains every day, and you will eliminate Wars and have universal Peace.

So he could see no particular Moral in writing an Introduction to my book, unless it was that Books should not depend entirely on their introductions as they do now. So I next thought of my friend Irvin Cobb. I had set next to him at so many Speakers Tables, at banquets, and had always given him any little extras that I might not want. Ice Cream and Sweets and things like that he just loves and ruins them at a Banquet. Well he was going Duck shooting down in Louisiana and said he wouldnt miss one Duck for the pleasure of writing the Introduction to the Encyclopedia Brittanica. So you just let the old fat thing try to get my Ice Cream at another Banquet.

Of course Ring Lardner was one of my very first thoughts, because I knew he could add the little touch of comedy that the book really needed. I went to him and told him that I only wanted something light and airy, maybe just one good joke would do the trick and take away from the serious nature of the Book. He is not only a Humorist but has got plenty money to show that he is. He said before he shook hands with me, What is there in it? I said well this is just a kind of an honorary thing, a kind of courtesy from one Author to another. He then asked me why should he give me a joke for nothing? He could put the joke into his Sunday Newspaper Article; then he could put the joke into his weekly Newspaper Cartoon; then he could sell it to a Musical Comedy and they would tell it so bad it would sound new. Then the Movies would buy it and make a drama out of it; then he would still hold the Phonograph, and broadcasting rights, and after it got well enough known write a Song around it. So he said I would be a fine egg to give you a joke for nothing.

I wish that Spaniard Ibanez, that wrote the 4

Horsemen was over here, I know him well, I had read 5 or 6 of his Books and I was to a big reception given to him in Los Angeles, and during our conversations through an Interpreter he learned I had read so many of his Books. No one else he met there even among the Literary ones had ever read any but the 4 Horsemen, So when he went home he sent me an Autographed Copy which read "To an American Cowboy, the only person in America I found who had read all my Books." The funny thing about it is that he is the only Author I ever read. Now if he was here he would write me an Introduction, But of course it would be in Spanish and nobody could read it, so I would be just as bad off as I am now.

I also know Elinor Glyn, I met her when she was out in California looking around for some one to cast as Paul in "Three Weeks." She sent for me but I had just started on another new Picture. She could have cooked me up a hot Introduction. She would have draped the first few paragraphs with Tiger skins, and described me in such a way that I would have really looked like something. So I just says to myself, why monkey with these writers, why not write my own Introduction? So here goes.

I have known Mr. Rogers for years and have long been familiar with his Literary masterpieces, both in Novels, and in Books of technical knowledge. I think there are few writers of Poetry or prose today who equal him, and I am certain he is surpassed by none.

I say this because I have lived and known the life he has pictured so well in this Book; I spent my late youth in these shaded oak lands where so many of his scenes are so pictorially laid, and he has made me live over again the scenes of my freshman manhood. No writer since the days of Remington can give you such a word picture of the west. That's because he is a westerner himself, and has only an eye for the beautiful things as he and nature alone can describe them. He alone of all our modern writers knows the people of which they write. When he describes a Corset you can feel it pinch. If it's a Sunrise he describes, you reach for an Umbrella. His jugglery of correct words and perfect English sentences is magical, and his spelling is almost uncanny.

The words, *Illiterate Digest,* which appear upon the title page of this book, has been generally compared to Don Quixote and to the Pickwick Papers, while E. M. Vogue places its author somewhere between Cervantes and LeSage. However, considerable the influence of Cervantes and Dickens may have been, the first in the matter of structure, the other in background, humor, and detail of characterization, the predominating and distinguishing quality of this Author's work is undeniably foreign to both and quite peculiar to itself. Something that for want of a better term might be called the quality of American Soul, any reader familiar as I know you all to be with the works of Dostoieffsky, Turgenev, or even Tolstoi, will grasp the deeper meaning of a work like this. Some consider the Author a realist, who has drawn with meticulous detail a picture of contemporary life, others more observing see in him a great symbolist.

He always remembers that it is dangerous to jest with laughter. This man in writing this has done a service to all thinking mankind. It is a revelation, as an omen of a freer future. Belinsky, the great Russian Critic to whom Mr. Rogers had read the manuscript, said "it looked like another Ben Hur to him."

So now Mr. Cobb, and Mr. Lardner, and all you introduction writers, what do I want with you?

There is not a one of you could have said the things of me that I have said, because you Guys dont know what books to look in to get all that big league stuff out of,

Yours for Arts sake,

William Penn Adair Rogers

(*boy that is my real name, let some Literary Guy top that*)

P. S. I got enough Introduction left over to write another Introduction if I had anything to write another book about.

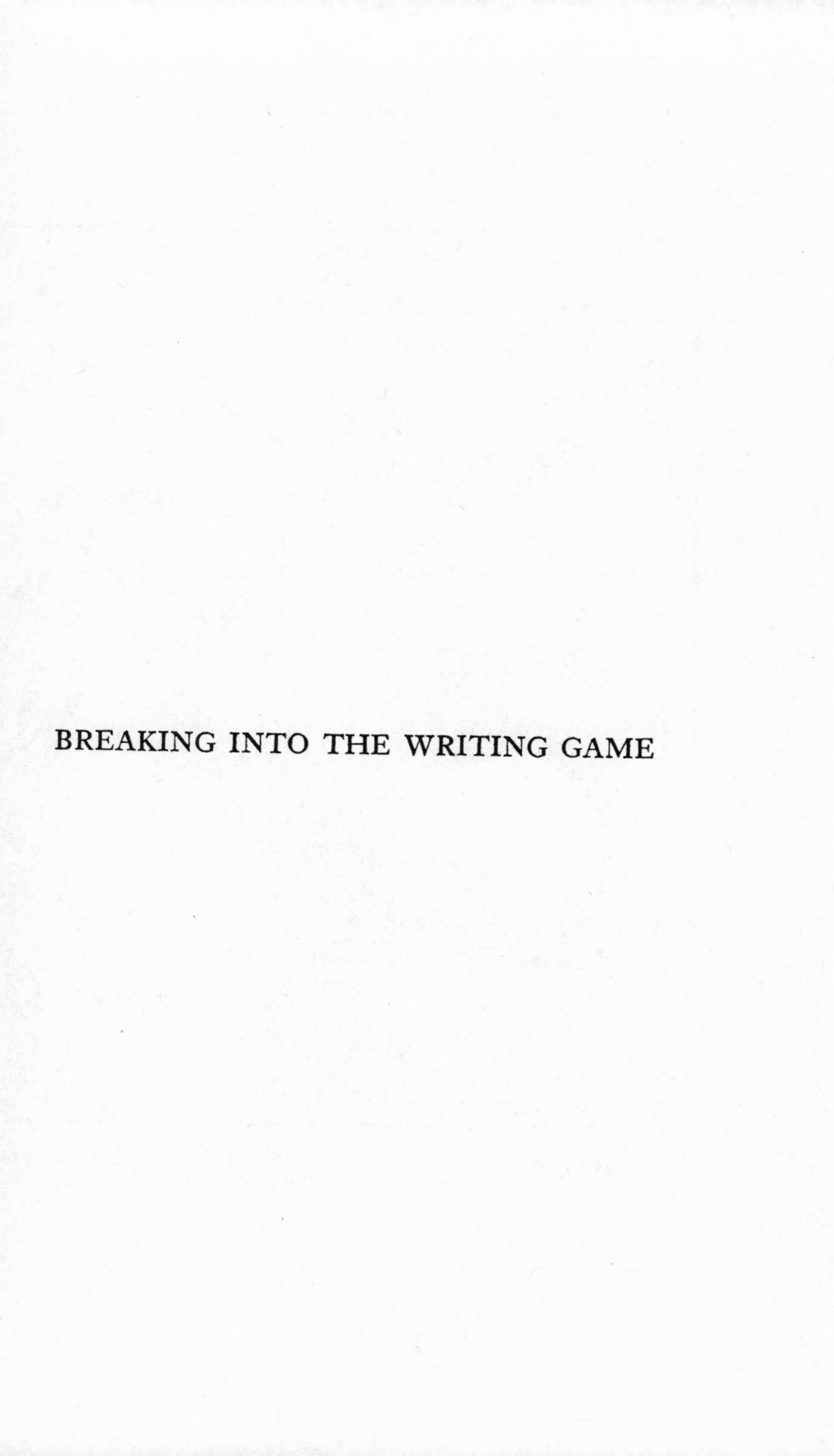

BREAKING INTO THE WRITING GAME

YOU ARE GOING TO GET THE LOW-DOWN ON SOME OF THOSE BIRDS WHO AR
SENDING HOME THE RADISH-SEED.

BREAKING INTO THE WRITING GAME

EVERYBODY is writing something nowadays. It used to be just the Literary or Newspaper men who were supposed to know what they were writing about that did all the writing. But nowadays all a man goes into office for is so he can try to find out something and then write it when he comes out.

Now being in Ziegfeld Follies for almost a solid year in New York has given me an inside track on some of our biggest men in this country who I meet nightly at the stage door.

So I am breaking out in a rash here. I will cite an example to prove to you what you are going to get. Not long ago there was a mess of Governors here from various Provinces. And a good friend of mine brought back to the stage and dressing room Governor Allen of Kansas. Well, I stood him in the wings and he was supposed to be looking at my act, but he wasn't. He was watching what really is the Backbone of our Show. He anyway heard some of my Gags about our Government and all who are elected to help missrun it.

So at the finish of my act I dragged him out on the stage and introduced him to the audience. He made a mighty pretty little speech and said he enjoyed Will's Impertinences, and got a big laugh on that. Said I was the only man in America who was able to tell the truth about our Men and Affairs.

When he finished I explained to the audience why I was able to tell the truth. It is because I have never mixed up in Politics. So you all are going from time to time to get the real Low Down on some of those Birds who are sending home the Radish Seed.

You know the more you read and observe about this Politics thing, you got to admit that each party is worse than the other. The one that's out always looks the best. My only solution would be to keep 'em both out one term and hire my good friend Henry Ford to run the whole thing and give him a commission on what he saves us. Put his factory in with the government and instead of Seeds every spring mail out those Things of his.

Mail Newberry one every morning Special Delivery.

Speaking of Henry Ford, I see where Uncle Henry has a new Rule in force out in his Factory where they paste those Knick Knacks together. Every man working there has to have his breath smelled every morning. That, of course, seems like a pretty strict Rule to put in force in a So called Free Country, and it has come in for a lot of criticism in the papers, but the way I look at it, it is absolutely necessary. Should a man go to work in there who had had a few strong shots of some of our National Drinks of today, he would blow his breath on one of those FOB'S, and blow all the bolts right out of it.

Now Mr. Ford is a very smart man and in passing these rigid rules I bet you he knows where to stop. I bet you that he won't instruct his Salesmen to be so strict with a Purchaser. In fact his salesmen smell of your breath when you come in to buy one and if it shows no signs of drink they don't try to sell you. He is smart enough to know a sober man would never buy one. Mind you, all this smelling of breath is done, not on the Company's time, but on the time of the Workers. Some men have to get up at 4 o'clock in the Morning to get their breath examined so they can get to work at 8. Imagine a line of 50 thousand all waiting to blow at a single individual TESTER! Think what he must be with all those Italian workmen passing by him. He is just 180 pounds of Garlic by night.

The University of Michigan is putting in a Chair in their Faculty devoted to the Art of Breath Detecting. But there is always a way to defeat any reform. Drinkers will learn to hold their breath like a Diver.

I tell you Folks, all Politics is Apple Sauce.

The President gave a Luncheon for the visiting Governors, where they discussed but didn't TRY Prohibition.

It was the consensus of opinion of all their speeches that there was a lot of drinking going on and that if it wasn't stopped by January that they would hold another meeting and try and get rid of some of the stuff.

Senator Curtis proposed a bill this week to stop Bootlegging in the Senate, making it unlawful for any member to be caught selling to another member while on Government property. While the bill was being read a Government employe fell just outside the Senate door and broke a Bottle of Pre-War Stuff (made just before last week's Turkish War). Now

THEY ARE CARPETING ALL THE HALLS OF THE SENATE SO IN CASE OF A FALL THERE WILL BE NO SERIOUS LOSS.

they are carpeting all the halls with a heavy material so in case of a fall there will be no serious loss.

Well, New Years is coming and I suppose we will have to hear and read all those big men's New Year greetings, such men as Schwab and Gary and Rockefeller and all of them. Saying the same old Apple Sauce. That they are Optimistic of the coming year and everybody must put their shoulder to the wheel, and produce more and they predict a great year. Say, if we had those Birds' Dough we could all be just as optimistic as they are. But it's a good Joke and it's got in the papers every year and I suppose always will.

Now the Ku Klux is coming into New York and kinder got it in for the Jewish People. Now they are wrong; I am against that. If the Jewish People here in New York City hadn't jumped in and made themselves good fellows and helped us celebrate our Christmas, the thing would have fell flat. They sold us every Present.

The Ku Klux couldn't get much of a footing here in New York. If there was some man they wanted to take out and Tar and Feather they wouldn't know where he lived. People move so often here their own folks don't know where they live.

And even if they found out the Elevator man in the Apartment wouldn't let 'em up.

See where there is bills up in Congress now to change the Constitution all around, elect the President in a different way and have Congress meet at a different time. It seems the men who drew up this thing years ago didn't know much and we are just now getting a bunch of real fellows who can take that old Parchment and fix it up like it should have been all these years. It seems it's just been luck that's got us by so far. Now when they get the Constitution all fixed up they are going to start in on the 10 Commandments, just as soon as they find somebody in Washington who has read them.

See where they are talking about another Conference over here. The Social Season in Washington must be lagging.

Well, I think they ought to have it. These Conferences don't really do any harm and they give certain Delegates pleasure. Of course nothing they ever pass on is ever carried out. (Except in Greece, where they are all carried out.) But each Nation gets a certain amount of Publicity out of it, and us masses that read of it get a certain amount of amusement out of it.

Borah himself admits he don't know what it's for or what they should do. But it looks like a good Conference season and there is no reason why we shouldn't get in on one.

BESIDES, DID YOU EVER REALIZE THIS COUNTRY IS 4 CONFERENCES BEHIND NOW?

I want to apologize and set my many readers straight as to why I am blossoming out as an infliction on you all.

It seems a prominent newspaper syndicate had Lloyd George signed up for a pack of his Memoirs. Well, after the late election Lloyd couldn't seem to remember anything, so they sent for me to fill in the space where he would have had his junk.

You see, they wanted me in the first place, but George came along and offered to work cheaper, and also to give his to charity. That benevolence on his part was of course before England gave him his two weeks' notice.

Now I am also not to be outdone by an ex-Prime Minister donating my receipts from my Prolific Tongue to a needy charity. The total share of this goes to the civilization of three young heathens, Rogers by name, and part Cherokee Indians by breeding.

Now, by wasting seven minutes, if you are a good reader—and ten to twelve if you read slow—on me, you are really doing a charitable act yourself by preventing these three miniature bandits from growing up in ignorance. So please help a man with not only one little Megan, but three little Megans.

A great many people may think that this is the first venture of such a conservative paper as the Illiterate Digest in using something of a semi-humorous nature, but that is by no means the case. I am following the Kaiser, who rewrote his life after it was too late. I realize what a tough job I have, succeeding a man who to be funny only had to relate the facts.

Please don't consider these as my memoirs. I am not passing out of the picture, as men generally are who write those things.

SETTLING THE CORSET PROBLEM OF THIS COUNTRY

(An After Dinner speech made at a Banquet of the Corset Manufacturers of America at the Waldorf-Astoria, New York.)

SETTLING THE CORSET PROBLEM OF THIS COUNTRY

SINCE I last wrote you all there has been an awful lot of fashion Shows and all their By Products held here in New York. All the out of Town buyers from all over have been here. So, on behalf of New York City, I had to help welcome them at their various Banquets. There was the retail Milliners' big fashion show at the Astor Ball Room where they showed 500 Hats and me. Some of the hats were just as funny looking as I was.

Well, I settled the Hat and Dress business to the satisfaction of everybody but the Milliners. So the next night at the Commodore Hotel I mingled with those Princes of Brigands, the Leather and Shoe men, and later I want to tell all you people just how they operate. For we never paid more for our Shoes and were nearer barefooted than we are today, so don't think that I am bought off this week by those Pasteboard Highbinders: it's only that I want to talk to the Ladies today.

During this reign of Indigestion I was called on

to speak at a big Banquet at the Waldorf to the Corset Manufacturers. Now that only shows you what a degrading thing this after Dinner speaking is. I want to get out of it in a few weeks and back to the Movies.

This speaking calls on a fellow to learn something about articles that a self-respecting man has no business knowing about. So that's why I am going to get away. If a Man is called on to tell in a Public Banquet room what he knows about Corsets, there is no telling what other Ladies' wearing apparel he might be called on to discuss. So me back to the Morals of Hollywood before it's too late.

I was, at that, mighty glad to appear at a dinner given by an essential Industry. Just imagine, if you can, if the flesh of this Country were allowed to wander around promiscuously! Why, there ain't no telling where it would wind up. There has got to be a gathering or a get-together place for everything in this world, so, when our human Bodies get beyond our control, why we have to call on some mechanical force to help assemble them and bring back what might be called the semblance of a human frame.

These Corset Builders, while they might not do a whole lot to help civilization, are a tremendous aid to the Eyesight. They have got what you would call a Herculean task as they really have to improve on nature. The same problem confronts them that does the people that run the Subways in New York City. They both have to get so many pounds of human flesh into a given radius. The subway does it by having strong men to push and shove until they can just close the door with only the last man's foot out. But the Corset Carpenters arrive at the same thing by a series of strings.

They have what is known as the Back Lace. This is known as a One Man Corset.

Now the Front Lace can be operated without a confederate. By judiciously holding your breath and with a conservative intake on the Diaphragm you arrange yourself inside this. Then you tie the strings to the door knob and slowly back away. When your speedometer says you have arrived at exactly 36, why, haul in your lines and tie off.

We have also the Side Lace that is made in case you are very fleshy, and need two accomplices to help you congregate yourself. You stand in the middle and they pull from both sides. This acts something in the nature of a vise. This style has been known to operate so successful that the victims' buttons have popped off their shoes.

Of course, the fear of every fleshy Lady is the broken Corset String. I sat next to a catastrophe of this nature once. We didn't know it at first, the deluge seemed so gradual, till finally the Gentleman on the opposite side of her and myself were gradually pushed off our Chairs. To show you what a wonderful thing this Corseting is, that Lady had come to the Dinner before the broken string episode in a small Roadster. She was delivered home in a Bus.

They have also worked out a second line of control, or a place to park an extra string on the back. You can change a string now while you wait, and they have demountable strings.

Now, of course, not as many women wear Corsets as used to but what they have lost in women they have made up with men. When corsets were a dollar a pair they used to be as alike as two Fords. A clerk just looked you over, decided on your circumference and wheel base and handed you out one. They come in long Boxes and you were in doubt at first if it was a Corset or a Casket.

Nowadays with the Wraparound and the Diaphragm-Control, and all those things a Corset Manufacturer uses more rubber than a Tire Co.

Imagine me being asked to talk at a Corset Dinner, anyway; Me, who has been six years with Ziegfeld Follies and not a Corset in the Show.

Men have gone down in History for shaping the destinies of Nations, but I tell you this set of Corset Architects shape the Destinies of Women and that is a lot more important than some of the shaping that has been done on a lot of Nations that I can name off hand. Another thing makes me so strong for them, if it wasn't for the Corset Ads in Magazines men would never look at a Magazine.

HOW TO TELL A BUTLER, AND OTHER ETIQUETTE

AS I OPENED THE DOOR TO LET HER IN 2 OF OUR DOGS AND 4 CATS CAME IN.

HOW TO TELL A BUTLER, AND OTHER ETIQUETTE

SOMEBODY must have seen me out in Public; I think it was Emily Post, for she sent me a book on ETIQUETTE that she had written herself.

It has 700 pages in it. You wouldn't think there was that much Etiquette, would you! Well, I hadn't read far when I found that I was wrong on most every line of the whole Book.

Now, you wouldn't think a Person could live under fairly civilized conditions (as I imagined I was doing) and be so dumb as to not have at least one of these forms of Etiquette right. Well, when I got through reading it, I felt like I had been a heathen all my life. But after I got to noticing other people I met I didn't feel so bad. Some of them didn't know much more about it than I did.

So I predict that her Book and all the other things you read now on Etiquette are going to fall on fertile soil. Now take, for instance, being introduced, or introducing someone; that is the first thing in the Book. I didn't know up to then that inflection of the voice was such a big factor in introductions.

She says that the prominence of the party being introduced determines the sound of the voice, as she says for instance, "Are you there?" and then on finding out you are there she says, "Is it raining?"

Now the inflection that you use on asking any one if they are there, is the same inflection that you are to use on introducing Mr. Gothis, if he is the more prominent of the two. Then for the other person, who Mr. Gothis probably got his from, why, you use the "Is it raining?" inflection.

You see, a fellow has to know a whole lot more than you think he does before he can properly introduce people to each other. First he has to be up on his Dunn and Bradstreet to tell which of the two is the more prominent. Second, he has to be an Elocutionist so he will know just where to bestow the inflection.

Well, I studied on that introduction Chapter till I thought I had it down pat. So I finally got a chance to try it out. My wife had invited a few friends for Dinner, and as she hadn't finished cooking it before they come, I had to meet them and introduce them to each other.

Well, I studied for half an hour before they come, trying to figure out which one was the most prominent so I could give her the "Are you there?" inflection. It was hard to figure out because any one of them couldn't be very prominent and be coming to our House for Dinner. So I thought, well, I will just give them both the "Is it raining?" inflection.

Then I happened to remember that the Husband of one of them had just bought a Drug Store, so I figured that I better give her the benefit of the "Are you there?" inflection, for if Prohibition stays in effect it's only a matter of days till her Husband will be prominent.

So, when they arrived I was remembering my opening Chapter of my Etiquette on Introductions. When the first one come I was all right; I didn't have to introduce her to anyone. I just opened our front door in answer to the Bell which didn't work. But I was peeping through the Curtains, and as I opened the door to let her in 2 of our Dogs and 4 Cats come in.

Well, while I was shooing them out, apologizing, and trying to make her believe it was unusual for them to do such a thing, now there I was! This Emily Post wrote 700 pages on Etiquette, but not a line on what to do in an emergency to remove Dogs and Cats and still be Nonchalant.

The second Lady arrived just as this Dog and Cat Pound of ours was emptying. She was the new Prescription Store Owner's Wife and was to get the "Are you there?" inflection. Her name was (I will call her Smith, but that was not her name). She don't want it to get out that she knows us.

Well, I had studied that Book thoroughly but those animals entering our Parlor had kinder upset me. So I said, "Mrs. Smith, Are you there? I want you to meet Mrs. Jones. Is it raining?"

Well, these Women looked at me like I was crazy. It was a silly thing to say. Mrs. Smith was there of course, or I couldn't have introduced her, and asking Mrs. Jones if it was raining was most uncalled for, because I had just looked out myself and, besides, any one that ever lived in California knows it won't rain again till next year.

But that didn't discourage me. I kept right on

learning and from now on I am just mangy with Etiquette.

Why, just the other day, I heard what I had always considered up to then a well behaved Woman, introduce one Gentleman friend to another and she said, "Allow me to present."

Now anybody that's ever read the first 5 lines in the book knows that the word Present is never used only on formal occasions. You should always say "May I introduce" on all informal occasions. There was a Woman who, to look at her, you would never have thought she could possibly be so rude and uncultured as to have made a mistake like that.

It just spoiled her for me. I don't care how many nice things she may do in the future, she just don't belong.

Rule 2, Chapter 5—: "No Gentleman under any circumstances chews Gum in Public." Now that kinder knocked me for a Goal, for I had been Chewing Gum before some of the best families in this Country. But from now on it is out. I am going to live according to the Book.

Chapter 6—: "Gentleman should not walk along the Street with their Cane or Stick striking the picket fence. Such habits should be curbed in the nursery."

Now that rule didn't hit me so hard for I am not lame and I don't carry a Cane yet, and furthermore, there is no Picket fences in California. If they had enough pickets to make a fence they would take them and build another Bungalow and rent it.

Outside of eating with a sharp knife, there is no rule in the Book that lays you liable to as much criticism as the following: "Whether in a private Car, a Taxi, or a carriage, a lady must never sit on a Gentleman's left, because according to European Etiquette a Lady 'on the left' is no lady."

I thought at first when I read that it was a misprint, and meant a Lady should never sit on a Gentleman's Lap, instead of Left. But now I find that it really was Left. So I guess you can go ahead and sit on the lap. It don't say not to. But don't sit on his Left, or you can never hope to enter smart society.

Then it says "the Owner of the car should always occupy the right hand side of the rear seat." No matter how many payments he has to make on it, that is considered his seat.

Chapter 7 is given over entirely to The Opera. What to wear, when to applaud—it tells everything

BIRDS THAT NEVER CAN TELL THE SERVANTS FROM THE GUESTS.

but how to enjoy the thing. The fellow that figures out how to enjoy the Opera in a foreign tongue, without kidding himself or fourflushing, has a fortune in store for him.

Chapter 12 tells how the Butler should dress. You don't know what a relief it was to me to find that news. I never had one, but if I do I will know what to costume him in.

The Book says: "At six o'clock the Butler puts on his dress Suit. The Butler's suit differs from that of a Gentleman by having no braid on his trousers."

Now all you Birds that never could tell the Servants from the Guests, except somebody called one of them a Butler and the other a Gentleman, you can't tell them that way. More than likely the Butler is the Gentleman of the two.

But I can tell the Butler. He has no braid on his trousers.

Now, all I got to do is find out how to tell the Gentleman.

If you see people walking around looking down at your trousers, in the future, you will know they are looking to see if the braid is left off.

DEFENDING MY SOUP PLATE POSITION

I WOULD INVENT A TRIANGLE SHAPE SLIDE THAT COULD BE PUSHED UNDER THE PLATE

DEFENDING MY SOUP PLATE POSITION

A COUPLE of weeks ago in my weekly Hamburger, I had the following, "If Mrs. J. W. Davis ever gets into the White House we will have a mistress to preside whom no titled European visitor can embarrass by doing the right thing first. She will never tip her Soup plate even if she can't get it all."

Now comes along an old friend of mine, Percy Hammond, a Theatrical Critic on a New York Paper (Pardon me, Percy, for having to tell them whom you are, but my readers are mostly provincial). He takes up a couple of columns, part of which follows:

"For years I have been tipping my Soup plate, but never until Mr. Rogers instructed me, did I know that I was performing a Social error. Consultation with the polished and urbane head waiters of the Middle West, where I spent my boyhood, taught me, I believed, to eat Soup. One wonders if Mr. Rogers has given as much thought to soup as he has to the Lariat. Perhaps he does not know, being recently from Oklahoma, that in many prominent eastern Dining rooms one may tip one's Soup plate, without losing his social standing. I regard Mr. Rogers' interference as prairie, impudent and unofficial. The Stewards of the Dutch Treat Club assure me that it is proper to tip one's plate, provided (and here is the subtlety that escapes Mr. Rogers), provided that one tips one's Soup plate from and not toward.

"Mr. Rogers might well observe the modesty in such matters that adorns Mr. Tom Mix his fellow ex-cowman. Mr. Mix, telling of a dinner given in his honor at the Hotel Astor, said, 'I et for two hours and didn't recognize a thing I et except an olive.' "

Them are Percy's very words. Now Percy (you notice I call you Percy, because if I kept saying, "Mr. Hammond, Mr. Hammond," all through my Article it might possibly appear too formal), Percy, I thought you were a Theatrical Critic. Now I find you are only a Soup Critic. Instead of going, as is customary, from soup to nuts, you have gone from Nuts to soup. Now, Percy, I have just read your Article on "my ignorance of Etiquette" (I don't know if that Etiquette thing is spelled right, or not; if it is not it will give you a chance for another

Article on my bad spelling). Now you do not have to write Articles on my lack of Etiquette, my ignorance, my bad English, or a thousand and one other defects. All the people that I ever met or any one who ever read one of my articles know that. That would be just like saying W. J. Bryan was in Politics just for Chatauqua Purposes. It's too well known to even comment on. Besides, I admit it.

Percy, I am just an old country boy in a big town trying to get along. I have been eating Pretty regular, and the reason I have been is because I have stayed an old country boy. Now I wrote that Article, and technically I admit I may have been wrong, but the Newspapers paid me a lot of money for it, and I never had a complaint. And by the way, I will get the same this week for writing about you that I did about Soup. Now both Articles may be wrong, But if you can show me how I can get any more money by writing them right, why I will split with you.

Now you took my soup article apart to see what made it float. I will see if we can't find some SMALL technicalities in your Literary Masterpiece. You say I came recently from Oklahoma, while You come from the Middle West and "by consultation with the Head Waiters have learned the proper way to eat soup." I thought Oklahoma was in the Middle West. Your knowledge of Geography is worse than my Etiquette. You say you learned to eat Soup from a Head Waiter in the Middle West. Well, I admit my ignorance again; I never saw a head waiter eat Soup. Down in Oklahoma (probably near Siberia) where I come from, we wouldn't let a head waiter eat at our Table, even if we had a head waiter, which we haven't. If I remember right I think it was my Mother taught me what little she knew of how I should eat, because if we had had to wait until we sent and got a head waiter to show us, we would have all starved to death. If a head waiter taught you to eat soup, Percy, I suppose you were sent to Bordens to learn how to drink Milk.

Then you state, "The Stewards of the Dutch Treat Club assure me that it is proper to tip one's plate." Now if you had learned properly from the great social Head Waiters of the urbane Middle West, why did you have to consult the Stewards of the Dutch Treat Club? Could it be that after arriving in N. Y. you couldn't rely on the information of the polished Head waiters of your phantom

Middle West? Now I was in the Dutch Treat Club once, but just as a Guest of Honor at a Luncheon, and of course had no chance to get into any intimate conversations with the Stewards. At that time, the place did not impress me as being where one might learn the last word in Etiquette.

And as for your saying that "anything of subtlety would escape me," that I also admit. I attribute it to my Dumbness. But as for me being too Dumb to get the idea of "the Soup plate being tipped away and not toward one," that's not Etiquette; that's just Self Protection. As bad as you plate tippers want all you can get, you don't want it in your lap. Custom makes manners, and while I know that it is permissible to tip plates, I still say that it is not a universal custom. Manners are nothing more than common sense, and a person has no more right to try and get every drop of soup out of his plate than he has to take a piece of bread and try and harvest all the Gravy in his plate. If you are that hungry, they ought to feed you out of a Nose Bag. So, "prairie impudence" or no "prairie impudence," I claim there are lots of them that don't do it, even if it is permissible (Head Waiters and Dutch Stewards to the contrary). It's permissible to get drunk but we still have a few that don't.

Now, Percy, suppose they all did as is permitted. Picture a big dinner with everybody with their soup plates all balanced up on edge, with one hand holding them up and the other hand with the spoon rounding up what little soup was left. They would resemble a lot of plate jugglers instead of Dinner Guests. Why if that was the universal custom, I would invent a triangle shape slide that could be pushed under the plate, so it would permit you to have one hand free, in case you were sitting next to your own wife, or if by chance you might want to use your napkin. According to your hungry plan, every Guest practically handcuffs himself during the latter end of the soup course. He is absolutely helpless. So don't ask head waiters and stewards what to do, Percy, look around yourself. You will find hundreds of them that are satisfied with just what Soup they can get on the level. Why I bet you are a fellow Percy, if you took Castor Oil, you would want to lick the spoon.

You know, Percy, I might know more about Etiquette than you think I do. I wrote a review on Emily Post's Book on Etiquette, and it was recopied in the Literary Digest (and by the way it did not mention the Digest's name, and it is unusual for them to re-copy anything unless they are mentioned in the article). Now have you or any of your Mid-Western head waiters, or retinue of Stewards, ever been asked to write a criticism on such an authoritative work as that? So you see I am somewhat of a Critic myself. I am the Hammond of the etiquette Book business.

Another thing, Percy, I spoke of a particular case; I mentioned Mrs. Davis. Well, I happened to see the Lady in question eat soup, and she did not try and corral the whole output. She perhaps knew it was permissible, still, she did not seem eager to take advantage of it.

Now, you speak of my friend, Tom Mix, where he says, "he et two hours and did not recognize anything he et but an olive." Now, that is bad Grammar, even I will admit, but it's mighty good eating. Don't you kinder envy him, that he has lived his life physically so that now he can eat for two hours. I bet you that you would trade your knowledge of the English language now for his constitution. Tipping that soup plate at all your meals for years is what put that front on you, Perc. Leave some, that's why I am trying to prove to you it's permissible to tip the plate, but it's bad physically. The fact that Tom has done something to be given a dinner for, should make him immune from attacks from the Press Table.

Vice Dawes, the profanity end of Coolidge's Campaign, just went through New York last week cussing everything, and everybody, a Hell'n Maria'ing all over the place. But he has other qualities to offset his cussing, so personally I don't think this word, "et" on Mix's part will seriously affect the drawing power of his pictures. You see, Percy, Tom said, "et," but you know better than him what to say. Still, if a Western Picture was to be made to amuse the entire World, I would trust Tom's judgment to yours. You know, Percy, everybody is ignorant, only on different subjects.

So, Perc, you string with the High Brows, but I am going to stick to the Low Brows, because I know I am at home with them. For remember, if it was not for us Low Brows, you high brows would have no one to discuss. But God love you, Percy, and if you ever want to leave them and come back to us where you started, we will all be glad to welcome you, even if you do feel like you are slumming. You must remember, Perc, that the question of the World today is, not how to *eat* soup, but how to *get* soup to eat.

HELPING THE GIRLS WITH THEIR INCOME TAXES

HELPING THE GIRLS WITH THEIR INCOME TAXES

WELL, I haven't had much time lately to dope out many new jokes. I have been helping the Girls in the Follies make out their Income Tax. A vital question come up, do Presents come under the heading of Salary? You know that's a mighty big item with us. When I say Us, I don't mean Me, as no one has given me anything yet, but I stick around in case a few crumbs drop.

I have been looking for a bribe from some of our prominent men to keep their name out of my act, but the only ones who even speak to me are the ones I mention. So I guess about the only way you can get a Man sore nowadays is to ignore him.

One Girl wanted to charge off Taxi Cab fares to and from the Theatre. I told her she couldn't do that. She said, "Well, how am I to get there?" I said, "Well, as far as the Government is concerned, you can come on the Subway." She said, "Oh! What is the Subway?"

Another Girl who has been with the various Follies for ten years wanted to know what She could charge off for Depreciation. And she was absolutely right because if, after being with them for that long, and you haven't married at least one Millionaire, you certainly have a legitimate claim for Depreciation.

I reminded one of the Girls that she had neglected to include two of her Alimony allowances. She said, "Do I have to put them all in?" I said, "Why, certainly you do." The Girl said, "Well, how did the Government keep track of them? I couldn't."

One Girl charged off a non-providing Husband under the heading of Bad Debts. We charged off all Cigarettes smoked in Public under the heading, Advertising.

One Sweetheart who paid for a Girl's Dinner every night, went thoroughly broke in Wall Street by trying to corner Canned Tomatoes in the late Piggledy-Wiggledy uprising. We figured up what the dinners would be for the rest of the year and charged him off as a Total Loss.

And right here I want to say what an honest bunch these Girls are. They don't want to beat the Government out of a thing. One Girl who had been away for a few weeks last winter to Palm Beach left a Husband in the good hands of her Girl Chum. When she returned the Girl Chum gave her a Two Thousand Dollar Bracelet. Now she wanted to include this Item in her Tax and we couldn't figure out where to put it. Finally we decided it was Rents, so we put it in, "For Rent, of One Husband, two Thousand Dollars."

Of course while the girls had these tremendous salaries I was able to help on account of my technical knowledge of them (as I dress with their Chauffeurs), and on account of my equal knowledge of making out an Income Tax, with any man in the World. As none of us know a thing about it.

Look what I saved them on Bathing Suits! I had them all claim they bought various Suits. And I defy even a Congressional Investigating Committee (and you certainly can't pick any more useless Body of men than they are), I defy them to say that a Bathing Suit on a Beautiful Girl don't come under the heading of Legitimate Advertising.

Now, as I say, these Girls all wanted to do what was right as they could afford to but this Income Tax has not acted that way with the Men. The

Income Tax has made more Liars out of the American people than Golf has.

Even when you make one out on the level, you don't know when it's through if you are a Crook or a Martyr.

Of course, people are getting smarter nowadays; they are letting Lawyers, instead of their conscience, be their Guide.

There is some talk of lowering it, and they will have to. People are not making enough to pay it.

And, by the way, the only way they will ever stop Bootlegging, too, is to make them pay an Income Tax. (At present it is a Tax exempt Industry.) Income Tax has stopped every other Industry, so there is no reason why it won't stop Bootlegging.

Of course, some of our more thrifty Girls have followed the example of their Male Tax Dodging friends and Incorporated (as the rate is lower on Corporations). Wall Street attended to that little matter when they were drawing the Tax Bill up in Washington.

These Girls had to do that, the same as men, to protect their Salaries. Of course, the big Gamble in buying into these Individual Corporations is the Lucky chance that she might make one or more wealthy marriages during the year. When of course, her being Incorporated, all she gets comes under the heading of Income, and you, as a Stockholder, get your Pro Rata Share. If she lands a big one you have struck Oil. Then, on the other hand, she may marry for love. In that case you have brought in a Duster.

For example, down on the Exchange you will find the Anastasia Reed, incorporated, along with General Motors and Blue Jay Corn Plasters. At the end of the year, the Stockholders, after adding up the Salary along with the accumulated Alimony, can either declare a dividend, or vote a Dinner and put the Undivided profits back into the growing Concern.

Now, I can't tell you the name but I was lucky enough to land 5 shares just before a Blonde Corporation married a Multi-Millionaire who was over 70 years of age. Us Stockholders have figured out at our last meeting that if he dies when we think he will (and we have no reason to believe otherwise, unless the Poison acts as a Monkey Gland) why, just those 5 shares will make me independent for life.

I don't want to use this space as an ad, but I

have been able for a small monetary fee to tip off my friends just what stock to buy. You see I am in a position to judge as I watch who is in the front row every night and I can just tell when Mendelssohn's Spring Song will start percolating for some particular Corporation. Now, at the present time, there is every night in the front row a Millionaire Oklahoma Oil Magnate and a Bootlegger, both angling for the same Corporation. If this Bootlegging person lands her, why her Stockholders are made for life, but if the Oil Magnate comes through (for sometimes these female Corporations are swayed by sentiment), why the stock won't be worth within a thousand Percent of what it will be if the Bootheel Party lands.

Now, take me personally; this Income Tax thing don't bother me at all. You are allowed 200 dollars for each Child, and my Children and my Income are just coming out even now.

THE GREATEST DOCUMENT IN AMERICAN LITERATURE

SONG WRITERS SHOULD BE SEGREGATED AND MADE TO SING THEIR SONGS TO EACH OTHER.

THE GREATEST DOCUMENT IN AMERICAN LITERATURE

THE subject for this brainy Editorial is resolved that, "Is the Song Yes We Have no Bananas the greatest or the worst Song that America ever had?"

I have read quite a lot in the papers about the degeneration of America by falling for a thing like it. Some lay it to the effects of Prohibition, some say it is the after-effects of War, that it is liable to follow every big war. I see where some have written editorials on the Song claiming that things are always in an unsettled state the year before a Presidential Election. I claim it's due to none of these causes at all; neither is it due to the French occupation of the Ruhr. I claim that it is the greatest document that has been penned in the entire History of American Literature.

And there is only one way to account for its popularity, and that is how you account for anything's popularity, and that is because it has Merit. Real down to earth merit, more than anything written in the last decade. The World was just hungry for something good and when this Genius come along and got right down and wrote on a subject that every Human being is familiar with, and that was Vegetables, Bologna, Eggs and Bananas, why he simply hit us where we live. You know a War Song will only appeal to people that are interested in war, a Love Song to those who are in love, A Mammy Song to nobody at all, but when you get down and write of Cabbages, Potatoes, and Tomatoes, you just about hit on a Universal subject.

You see, we had been eating these things all our lives but no one had ever thought of paying homage to them in Words and Harmony. It opens up a new field for Song Writers. I look for an epidemic of Corned Beef, Liver and Bacon, Soup and Hash Songs to flood the Market. So more power to an originator. Did you ever stop to realize that that Song has attracted more attention than anything that has taken place in this Country since Valentino gave up the screen for a mud Face preparation?

Magnus Johnson of Wisconsin or Minnesota (they ought to put those States together; nobody can ever remember which one anything ever happens in, generally the same thing happens in both of them); well as I say, Magnus was unfortunate enough to be elected to the United States Senate at a time when Bananas was at its height. Ten thousand people can sing the song that dont know that Magnus can milk a Cow with one hand and broadcast a Political speech with the other. Millions can hum the Song that cant tell you what Lloyd George is sore at England about.

Hiram Johnson arrived from Europe a Presidential possibility, and spoke to 2 thousand people. The creator of Bananas to Music, penned one Gem of constructive thought, and spoke not to two thousand but to one hundred and ten million.

Then some Editorial Newspaper writer has the nerve to sneer at this marvelous Song, when perhaps his writings never cross the County line. Why, Italy has already made arrangements on account of his honoring their National Diet to place his name alongside of Michael Angelo, Garibaldi, and Louis Firpo. It is already bringing on International complications. England is sore because he didn't say something about Tea and Cake.

If we had had a Man like that to write our National Anthem somebody could learn it. It wouldn't take three wars to learn the words.

Mother has been done to death in Songs and not enough consideration shown her in real life. We thought when we sang about her we had paid her all the respect there was. I tell you, conditions were Just Ripe for a good fruit Song.

Geo. M. Cohan wore out more Flags than a war waving them to music. He transferred the Flag from Cloth to Paper, he made it a two verse and Chorus affair. Now George was original. He saw an idea; he knew that a big percentage of the American people had seen the flag, so that would give him a subject to write on that people knew about. But look what a Universal subject this Bird hit on. There are thousands of Foreigners landing here daily that know Spin-ISH and HON-ions, that dont know an American Flag from a Navajo Blanket.

Did you ever just dissect the Words to some of our so-called Popular Songs? One has the words "Its not raining Rain, its raining Violets." Now can you imagine any more of a Cuckoo idea than that? You cant hardly raise the things, much less Rain em. Now which do we owe the most to, the Violet or the Banana? Even such a Genius as Geo. M. Cohan himself has a Song, "You remind me of my Mother when Mother was A Girl like you." How can any man remember his Mother when she was a girl? Its a Physical impossibility. You would have had to be born almost simultaneously with your Mother.

Now on the other hand take the Banana Classic. "We just killed a Pony so try our Bologna, It's flavored with Oats and Hay." Now that's not only good Poetry but his honesty should be rewarded. He is on the level, he is telling you just what you get. Then those History-making lines, "Our Hen Fruit have you tried em, real live Chickens inside em." Now I think in the rhyming line that is a positive Gem, and will live when Gungha Din has lost his Hot Water Bottle. That shows originality. He is not just simply going along rhyming Girl and Pearl, Beauty and Cutey, Bees and Knees.

This Boy has got the stuff. Get this one and then read all through Shakespeare and see if he ever scrambled up a mess of words like these, "Try our Walnuts and Co- CO- Nuts, there aint many nuts like They." Now just off-hand you would think that it is purely a commercial Song with no tinge of Sentiment, but dont you believe it. Read this: "And you can take home for the WIM-mens, nice juicy per-Sim-mons." Now that shows thoughtfulness for the fair sex and also excellent judgment in the choice of a Delicacy. Then there is rhythm and harmony that would do credit to a Walt Whitman, so I defy you to show me a single song with so much downright merit to it as this has.

You know, it dont take much to rank a man away up if he is just lucky in coining the right words. Now take for instance Horace Greeley, I think it was, or was it W. G. McAdoo, who said "go West, young man." Now that took no original thought at the time it was uttered. There was no other place for a man to go, still it has lived. Now you mean to tell me that a commonplace remark like that has the real backbone of this one: "Our Grapefruit I'll bet you, Is not going to wet you, we drain them out every day." Now which do you think it would take you the longest to think of, that or "Go West, Young Man."

Some other fellow made himself by saying "War is Hell." Now what was original about that? Anyone who had been in one could have told you that, and today he has one of the biggest Statues in

New York. According to that, what should this Banana man get? He should be voted the Poet Lariet of America.

Now mind you, I am not upholding this man because I hold any briefs for the Songwriters. I think they are in a class with the After Dinner speakers. They should be like Vice used to be in some towns. *They should be segregated off to themselves* and not allowed to associate with people at all, *and should be made to sing these songs to each other.* That is the only way you will ever do away with the Song writing business.

Another thing that has made it bad is these People that used to send Scenarios to Moving Picture Studios, after getting them back have turned them into Songs. Its been a Godsend to the Picture business but a blow to the Music business. And those Mammy Songs—those writers should have all been banished to Siberia, and as they went through on their way to Siberia dont let them stop in Russia to see their Mammy. But when one does come along and display real talent as this one has proven, I think he should be encouraged. Some man said years ago that he "cared not who fought their Countries' Wars as long as he could write their Songs." But of the two our Songs have been the most devastating.

I understand this Boy was a Drummer in a Jazz Band before this World renown hit him. Now I personally have always considered the Drummer the best part of the Jazz Band. I think if all the members of a Jazz band played the Drums it would make better music. I would rather have been the Author of that Banana Masterpiece than the Author of the Constitution of the United States. No one has offered any amendments to it. Its the only thing ever written in America that we haven't changed, most of them for the worst.

PROSPECTUS FOR "THE REMODELED CHEWING GUM CORPORATION"

WHY CAN'T I DO SOMETHING WITH SECOND-HAND GUM?

PROSPECTUS FOR "THE REMODELED CHEWING GUM CORPORATION"

LAST week I made, on account of my Movie work, a trip to Catalina Island and along with the Glass bottom Boat I had pointed out to me the home of Mr. William Wrigley on the top of the highest mountain. He also owns the Island. We were not allowed to go nearer than the gate as the Guide said some other Tourist had carried away a Grand Piano, and he had gotten discouraged at having them around. Another tourist was caught right on the Lawn Chewing an opposition Brand of Gum. That is really the thing that gummed up the Tourist Parade.

Then I remembered having seen his wonderful building in Chicago, all, mind you, accumulated on Chewing Gum at a Cent a Chew. Now I felt rather hurt at not being allowed to at least walk through maybe the Kitchen, or the Cellar, because I know that I have contributed more to the Building of that Home than any one living. I have not only made Chewing Gum a pastime but I have made it an Art. I have brought it right out in

Public and Chewed before some of the oldest Political Families of Massachusetts.

I have had Senator Lodge (who can take the poorest arguments in the World and dress them up in perfect English and sell them) after hearing my Act on the Stage, say: "William" (that's English for Will), "William, I could not comprehend a word of the Language you speak, but you do Masticate uncompromisingly excellent."

This reception which I received at the Wrigley Home was so in contrast to the one which I received at Mr. Adolphus Busch's in St. Louis. When he heard that one of his best Customers was at the outer Gate, Mr. Busch not only welcomed me, but sent me a fine German Police Dog to California, the stock of which had come direct from the Kaiser's Kennels in Pottsdam. The Dog did wonderful until some one here by mistake gave him a drink of Half of One Percent Beer. He would have been six years old next May.

After looking on Mr. Wrigley's home with much admiration and no little envy, the thought struck me: A man to succeed nowadays must have an Idea. Here I am, struggling along and wasting my time on trying to find something nice to say of our Public Men, when I should be doing Something with Dividends connected with it. So then the thought struck me: WHAT BECOMES OF ALL THE CHEWING GUM THAT IS USED IN THIS COUNTRY?

I just thought to myself, if Bill Wrigley can amass this colossal fortune, and pay the Manufacturing charges, why can't I do something with Second Hand Gum. I will have no expense, only the accumulation of the Gum after it is thoroughly masticated. Who would be the most beneficial to mankind, the man who invented Chewing Gum, or me who can find a use for it? Why, say, if I can take a wad of old Gum and graft it onto some other substance, I will be the modern Burbank. (With the ideas I have got for used Gum I may be honored by my Native State of Oklahoma by being made Governor, with the impeachment clause scratched out of the Contract.)

All Wrigley had was an Idea. He was the first man to discover that the American Jaws must wag. So why not give them something to wag against? That is, put in a kind of Shock Absorber.

If it wasn't for Chewing Gum, Americans would wear their teeth off just hitting them against each other. Every Scientist has been figuring out who the different races descend from. I don't know about the other Tribes, but I do know that the American Race descended from the Cow. And Wrigley was smart enough to furnish the Cud. He has made the whole World chew for Democracy.

That's why this subject touches me so deeply. I have chewed more Gum than any living Man. My Act on the Stage depended on the grade of Gum I chewed. Lots of my readers have seen me and perhaps noted the poor quality of my jokes on that particular night. Now I was not personally responsible for that. I just happened to hit on a poor piece of Gum. One can't always go by the brand. There just may be a poor stick of Gum in what otherwise may be a perfect package. It may look like the others on the outside but after you get warmed up on it, why, you will find that it has a flaw in it. And hence my act would suffer. I have always maintained that big Manufacturers of America's greatest necessity should have a Taster —a man who personally tries every Piece of Gum put out.

Now lots of People don't figure the lasting quality of Gum. Why, I have had Gum that wouldn't last you over half a day, while there are others which are like Wine—they improve with Age.

I hit on a certain piece of Gum once, which I used to park on the Mirror of my dressing room after each show. Why, you don't know what a pleasure it was to chew that Gum. It had a kick, or spring to it, that you don't find once in a thousand Packages. I have always thought it must have been made for Wrigley himself.

And say, what jokes I thought of while chewing that Gum! Ziegfeld himself couldn't understand what had put such life and Humor into my Work.

Then one night it was stolen, and another piece was substituted in its place, but the minute I started in to work on this other Piece I knew that someone had made a switch. I knew this was a Fake. I hadn't been out on the Stage 3 minutes until half of the audience were asleep and the other half were hissing me. So I just want to say you can't exercise too much care and judgment in the selection of your Gum, because if it acts that way with me in my work, it must do the same with others, only they have not made the study of it that I have.

Now you take Bryan. I lay his downfall to Gum.

You put that man on good Gum and he will be parking it right under the White House Dinner Table.

Now, some Gum won't stick easy. It's hard to transfer from your hand to the Chair. Other kinds are heavy and pull hard. It's almost impossible to remove them from Wood or Varnish without losing a certain amount of the Body of the Gum.

There is lots to be said for Gum. This pet Piece of mine I afterwards learned had been stolen by a Follies Show Girl, who two weeks later married an Oil Millionaire.

Gum is the only ingredient of our National Life of which no one knows how or of what it is made. We know that Sawdust makes our Breakfast food. We know that Tomato Cans constitute Ford Bodies. We know that old Second-hand Newspapers make our 15 dollar Shoes. We know that Cotton makes our All-Wool Suits. But no one knows yet what constitutes a mouthful of Chewing Gum.

But I claim if you can make it out of old Rubber Boots and Tires and every form of old junk, why can't I, after reassembling it, put it back into these same Commodities? No one has found a substitute for Concrete. Why not Gum? Harden the surface so the Pedestrians would not vacate with your street. What could be better for a Dam for a River than old Chewing Gum? Put one Female College on the banks of the Grand Canyon, and they will Dam it up in 2 years, provided they use discretion in their parking.

Now, as for my plans of accumulation, put a Man at every Gum selling place. The minute a Customer buys, he follows him. He don't have to watch where he throws it when through; all he has to do is to follow. He will step on it sooner or later no matter where they throw it.

When he feels it, he immediately cuts off the part of the shoe where it is stuck on, so he can save the entire piece. Then he goes back and awaits another buyer.

I have gone into the matter so thoroughly that I made a week's test at a friend of mine's Theatre. At one of Mr. Sid Grauman's Movie Theatres here, I gathered gum for one week and kept account of the intake every day. My statistics have proven that every Seat in every Movie Theatre will yield a half Pint of Gum every 2 days, some only just slightly used.

Now that gives us an average of a Pint and a

Half every six days, not counting Sunday where the Pro Rata really increases. Now figure the seating capacity of the Theatre and you arrive at just what our Proposition will yield in a good solid commodity.

Of course, this thing is too big for me to handle personally. I can, myself, disrobe, after every Show, one Theatre and perhaps a Church on Sunday. But to make it National I have to form it into a Trust. We will call it the "Remodeled Chewing Gum Corporation."

Don't call it Second Hand; there is no Dignity in that name. If we say "remodeled" why every Bird in America falls for that.

Of course, it is my idea ultimately after we have assembled more than we can use for Concrete and Tires and Rubber Boots to get a Press of some kind and mash it up in different and odd shapes.

(You know there is nothing that takes at a Dinner like some Popular Juice Flavor to our Remodeled and overhauled Product. I would suggest Wood Alcohol. That would combine two Industries into one.)

I want to put flavors in there where we can take some of this colossal trade away from these

Plutocratic Top Booted Gentlemen. If we can get just enough of this Wood Alcohol into our reassembled Gum to make them feel it and still not totally destroy our Customer we will have improved on the Modern Bootlegger as he can only sell to the same man once.

Now, Gentlemen and Ladies, you have my proposition. Get in early on, "Old Gum made as good as New." Think of the different brands that would be popular, "Peruna Flavor Gum," "Jamaica Ginger Gum," "Glover's Mange Gum," "Lysol Gum."

It looks like a great proposition to me. It will be the only Industry in the World where all we have to do is to just pick it up, already made, and flavor it.

I am going to put this thing up to my friend, Henry Ford. Think, with no overhead, how he could keep the Cost down. It's a better proposition than being President.

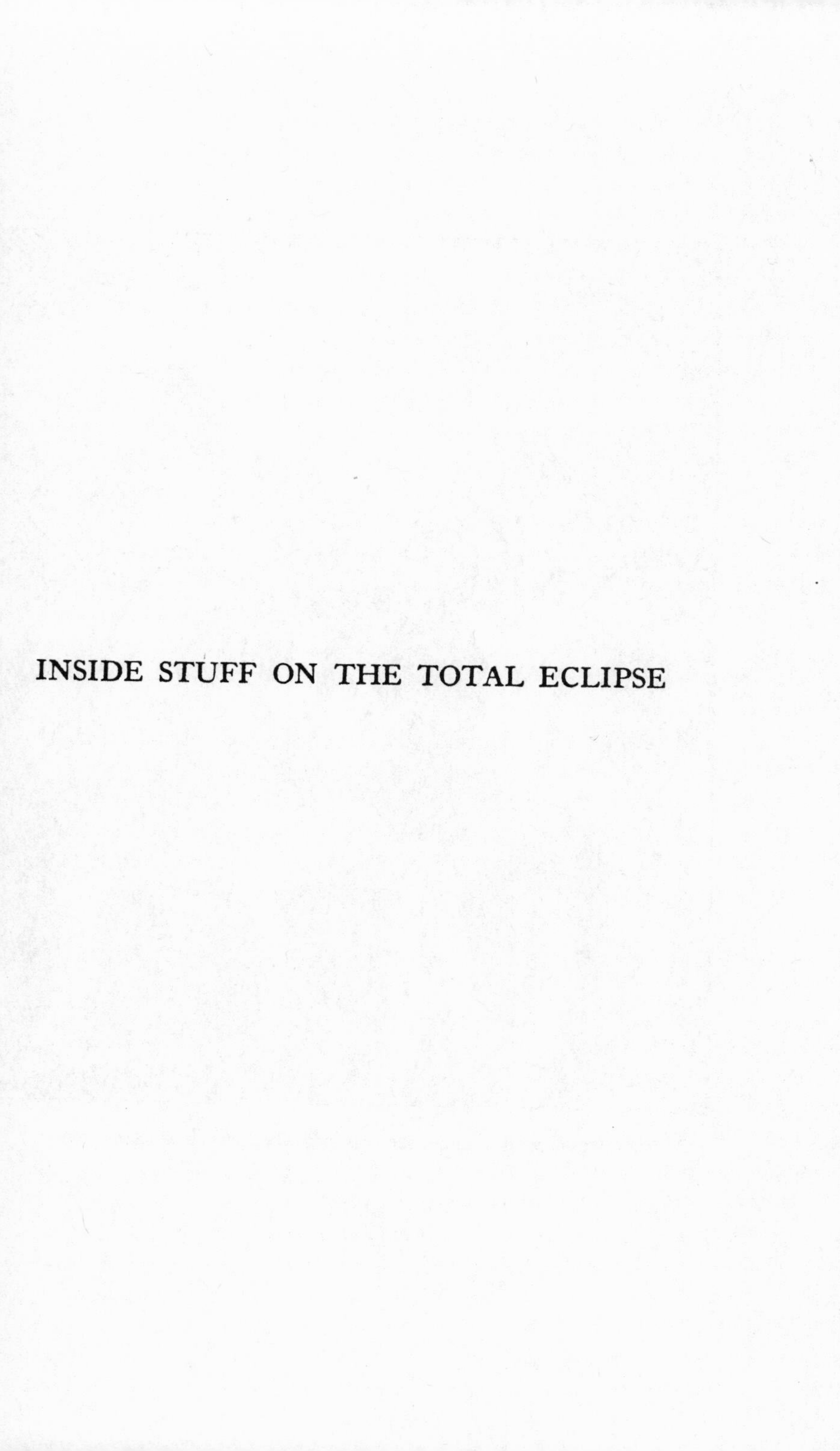

INSIDE STUFF ON THE TOTAL ECLIPSE

THE MORE GLASSES YOU USED THE MORE ECLIPSE YOU COULD SEE.

INSIDE STUFF ON THE TOTAL ECLIPSE

WELL, I have just this minute returned from Tia Juana, Mexico, where I along with some thousands of other Scientists went to observe the Total Eclipse. That is that was their excuse for going. You know it don't take much excuse to get a man, or Woman either, to go to Mexico nowadays. So when the Scientists said that Los Angeles was only to get a 99 percent Eclipse, (That is about the only thing I ever knew Los Angeles to fall down on. They are generally 100 percent) it kinder hurt their pride. It was the first time that Nature had ever handed them a mere 99.

I don't really think they would have ever gotten over it but San Francisco only received some 85 or 90 percent so that kinder salved things over.

But the Chamber of Commerce has held a meeting and voted Resolutions to apply for the next Eclipse in its entirety. They claim that it was due to the Club not giving the matter more thought that they lost the One Percent on this one.

Well, the Scientist Road Map showed that Catilina Island and San Diego and Tia Juana, were right in the path of total blackness. Everybody that could get out of a Cafeteria line in time to make the trip started for one of these places. Catilina Island offered wonderful possibilities. You could get two rounds of Seasickness, see the Eclipse and get your Chewing Gum at cost—all in one day's pleasure.

San Diego is a Town built in the most South Westerly part of the United States where Americans who are coming out of Mexico sober up, before being able to go to their various homes, and it is really remarkable what a thriving Town it is. You would be surprised at the business they do.

There are nice Hotels there with Ice Water in every room, and even Banks where you can draw Drafts on your Home Bank after a Day in Mexico at the Tables (as they say in Monte Carlo books). San Diego catches very few going down into Mexico, (only the Punctures) as most People are in a great hurry to get there, once you begin to reach this Oasis.

So you see it didn't take much decision on my part to decide that if I, along with the other Scientists who were to write on this Traffic accident in the Skies, wanted to pick out an observatory there was no particular reason why we should select a Dry one.

Well, my friend Mr. Henry Ford may or may not ever be President, but I want to publicly say this to him, that the people he sells his Cars to are of a very high type of intelligence. I never saw so many owners of one make of car so interested in Astronomy in my life. There were not only Autos of every make but people of every make, jammed two rows deep for 150 miles struggling to reach Tia Juana, Mexico FOR THE ECLIPSE.

You would see people going to Mexico to see this eclipse, who, if you looked at them, you wouldn't think they knew when Sunday passed between Monday and Saturday, much less when the Moon passed between the Sun and Earth.

Now, as I say, we passed through some 70 miles of United States Territory that was to be blotted out totally, but there wasn't an observatory in the entire region. Being my first year as a Journalist and this being my first assignment to cover a total Eclipse for the various papers who crave my Scientific knowledge, I am really ashamed to admit it, but, outside of not even knowing what an Eclipse was or when one was to happen, I had never even entered one of their Observatories where they watch these Eclipses; so it was with the greatest anxiety and enthusiasm that I dashed up to the Mexico line.

The Country to the south of us we have lately recognized. (The receipt for any other Nation that wants us to recognize them, is to strike Oil, or some other commodity that our Capitalists want.) But this editorial is not on our Foreign Relations. That I will take up in due time as we have some Foreign Relations. This is to be on the Planets, their various Routes, mode and speed of travel.

A great many Scientists, I had read in the papers, were bringing Cameras to Photograph this remarkable phenomenon. But most of the Scientists that I saw had Jugs and Flasks. Well, not being up on Science, I didn't know what to bring. You know these Scientists are such a queer lot I wouldn't be surprised at anything they do.

Well, I asked the Custom Inspector where the Observatory was. He said, "Which one?" I said, "Lick." (That was the only one I had ever heard of.) He said, "Right over there is one, if it ain't all Licked up."

You never saw such an accommodating Country in the World. Just think the preparations they had gone through for the visiting Scientists' Pleasure. They had built these Observatories all over the place right up to the line where you would lose no time. You could start observing the minute you got into the Country.

Now, there is apt to be among my readers some who are as ignorant as I was about the inside of an Observatory, so for their benefit I will explain just what it is like. On the left, as you enter, is a long Table affair, that runs the length of the room. It's really higher than a Table, and back of it is a long Mirror where you get the reflections of any local Eclipses that might happen. Then on the bottom, outside this high counter, is a little low railing that Singers' Midgets could look over if they wanted to see an Eclipse.

Now, up here in Los Angeles, they talked about smoked Glasses, but down there they just filled them and looked through them, and the more Glasses you used, and the more different kinds of glasses, why, the more Eclipse you could see. Some men would have to get the man to let them try a dozen different Glasses before they could get the right Focus.

Then, on the other side of the room, if you didn't want to look through glasses upside down, why they had various other instruments of knowledge. One was a Table with little Cubes cut square (or apparently square) with Dots on them and the Scientist would shake them in his hand and lay down some Money, and then let them empty out his hand. Then another Scientist, even more of a Scientist, would pick up the money in one hand and the little squares in the other and hand the squares to another Scientist and put the money in his Pocket. Then the same operation would be gone through, till each Scientist, except the good one, would be Gone Through.

I asked a visiting Astronomy Professor what the idea was. He said, "You can see if you are right." I says, "What has that got to do with the eclipse?" He says, "Why you bet on the passing." So I bet him I would pass but I didn't, so now I want the Scientist to figure out in what year I am going to pass.

By that time it was 12.50 P. M. so I come out of the Observatory as that was the time it was supposed to be Total, but there wasn't a Soul on the Streets or outside any place. Everybody was on the inside looking at the Eclipse. It was pretty dark on the Street and a Mexican who lived in the edge of the Town started milking his Cow, and raising the mischief with his wife because she didn't have his supper ready.

One fellow staggered out of an Observatory and I asked him if he had seen the Eclipse and he said, "Which one?" But it certainly was a success from a Scientific point of view, for away along in the evening after it had gotten light, I saw Astronomers piled up in every Observatory just overcome by what the Scientists call the Corona, or after effects of an Eclipse.

Oh yes, the Mexicans also put on for the visiting Astrologers a Bull Fight. It was held at the lower end of the Town. You had to pass every Observatory in town before you reached the Bull Ring.

Well, I went down and there was lots of Natives but very few Americans. As I say, it was held at the wrong end of the Town for them to reach it. I guess it was the only Fight ever held during an Eclipse.

Can you imagine getting in a Pen with a Bull in

the dark. I wouldn't even get in with one in the light. Well, the Bulls turned out to be Steers. I guess on account of the Eclipse and the Condition the Americans would be in, the Mexicans figured they wouldn't know the difference. They didn't kill the Bulls, and the Bulls wasn't lucky enough to do any damage themselves. As a strict Humane man I could see nothing to kick about, only from an audience's standpoint.

So I left Tia Juana and come back to this side where everybody had looked at the Eclipse from out of doors, and they all seemed to be kinder disappointed. It didn't do anything. You see from the amount of Press stuff written about it most people kinder thought it would do some tricks, maybe juggle or shimmy or something like that. It just passed—that's all. I, personally, along with all the others couldn't see anything so wonderful about it's doing that. If the two planets hadn't passed but had hit, that would have been something to see.

Of course, I will admit in this day of congested Traffic, for any two given objects to meet and pass without hitting is considered wonderful.

Everybody I talked with seemed to be unanimous

that they would rather have seen the Dempsey and Firpo fight. So I guess that is why they only have Eclipses every 100 years so they won't have to draw from the same crowd twice.

But no one who saw it from Mexico had any fault to find with it at all. If there is any great thing happening and you are not right sure you will enjoy it, why, go to Mexico and see it.

I tell you a thing looks different from a foreign country. I wish I could have seen the Democratic and Republican Conventions from Tia Juana.

The Eclipse was kinder overrated but I tell you Mexico ain't.

IT'S TIME SOMEBODY SAID A WORD FOR CALIFORNIA

(A speech delivered impromptu at a Dinner to the Old Settlers of California. Mr. Rogers had another speech prepared but when he found everybody boosting California he changed his speech.)

I JUST HAPPENED TO REMEMBER THAT NO ONE HAD SAID A WORD FOR CALIFORNIA.

IT'S TIME SOMEBODY SAID A WORD FOR CALIFORNIA

I ATTENDED a dinner the other morning given for the Old Settlers of California. No one was allowed to attend unless he had been in the State 2 and one-half years.

I was the last speaker on the Menu. They put me last, figuring everybody would either be asleep or gone by the time I began.

Well sir, do you know, by the time it got to me there was nothing left to talk on! But I just happened to notice that in all the other speeches no one had mentioned California, so as that was all I had left I just had to go ahead and do the best I could with California.

Now, it ain't much of a speech but it is at least a novelty, because in all my time out here I had never heard the subject used before at any Dinners or Luncheons.

Mr. Toastmaster, Ladies and Gentlemen, and Members of the Old California Settlers Association: Your previous speakers have taken up so much time boosting and praising other States and their People that it is now most daylight, and I am at a loss to pick a subject, but at the last minute I just happened to remember that no one had said a word for California. So I will take up this very remote subject and see if I can't do something to drag it out of the obscurity in which it has been placed here tonight.

Being one of your old Timers (I have been a resident of this State now for nearly 4 years; there is only one other older member in the organization) I want to say right here that you often hear it said, "What is the matter with California?" Well, I will tell you what is the matter—it's MODESTY, that's what it is, too much MODESTY.

If we got out and blew our own Horns and Advertised and boosted our State like Delaware, and Rhode Island have, we wouldn't be so little heard of. So, whether you like it or not fellow Statesmen, I for one am going to throw Modesty to the winds and just tell the World off-hand a few of the things that we have got out here.

Now, just picking subjects at random, what do you suppose we could do if we wanted to say something about CLIMATE? Why, that item alone would draw people here. But what do we do?

We just set here and say nothing. We go out of the State and we are so darn generous that all we do is brag on the place where we are. We never think of handing our own State a little free advertising.

But you take, as I say, a fellow from Delaware, and he is preaching Delaware and all its advantages from the time you meet him till you leave him, and by golly, it pays to do that. Look at Delaware today! So never mind this old good fellow spirit of giving the other fellow the best of it. I believe in throwing in a little boost for the old Native Heath.

Now I know you other members don't agree with me and think that we should think of our proud traditions and not stoop so low as to have to advertise but I tell you that this day and time is a commercial Age, and we have got to throw our Pride away and let the World know just what we have here.

There is no reason why other People from neighboring States shouldn't know of our Climate. Why keep it hid? It's here. We got it. They can't take it away with them.

Of course, I will admit that we have done a

little good in a small way with Picture Post Cards. Five years ago Iowa was a prosperous and satisfied State. They had no idea of leaving. They had shoveled snow for 5 months every year and figured they would always shovel snow 5 months every year. But finally one day a Twenty Dollar Bill come into the State and a Farmer wanted to get change for it, so he started out trying to get it changed and wound up in Long Beach, California.

A fellow selling Roses in January changed it for him, and when the Farmer pulled off his Mittens to count the change he found that it was warm and he didn't have to put the mittens back on again. That made quite a hit with him and he decided to stay awhile. So he sent a Picture Post Card back with the Picture of a Man Picking Oranges off the trees in January, and told them how fine it was and everybody that read the Post Card, including the Postmaster come on out.

So when they came they sent back Picture Post Cards to all their Friends who liked Oranges, and in time they came too, and so on, each newcomer bringing out just as many more as he could afford Post Cards. Now in the short space of 5 years look what has happened. The whole of the State of Iowa is here. The only ones left back there are the ones who can't read the Post Cards, or People who don't care for Oranges, and now I see where they have put in Schools to teach those others to read so that means we will eventually have them all, with the exception of the ones who don't like Oranges.

Now, as I say, if all of that can be done with just Picture Post Cards, what do you suppose could have been done if the Newspapers of our State had thought to have said something in praise of our Climate? So, Fellow Old Timers, if we can get the grand State of Iowa out here on a Picture Post Card of an Orange Tree, what could we do with some of these other States if we really devoted a little of our time to it!

Why, Oranges are a small time commodity with us. We raise more Beans on one farm here without Irrigating than we do Oranges in the whole State. If we had Picture Post Cards of Bean Fields instead of Orange Fields we could get the whole of Boston here the same as we did with Iowa. You will do even better with Boston than you did with Iowa because everybody there likes Beans.

So let's get busy and let them know what we are doing in the Bean line.

Take the case of Oil. You all know we struck Oil here in Southern California. But did you let anybody else know it? No, you didn't say a word about it, and as a consequence, a man can't even find a place to buy an Oil Stock. Now there are lots of People would buy shares and Units, but no, you are so darn MODEST you won't let the World know what we have.

I would like to have seen what Delaware would have done if they had found this much Oil. They would have sold so much Stock that if the Pacific Ocean had been Oil it wouldn't have paid back the Buyers.

Look at Real Estate. Here we have the greatest Land and Lots that ever laid out of doors, but do we do anything with them? No! We just set here. We never advertise them; we never boost them. I wish you could see what the State of Delaware would do if they had the same class of lots that we have here. Why they would have Sub-Divisions all over the place. They would have Barbecues, and Drawings, and Scream Stars personally appearing, and men under umbrellas selling each lot. But no, we are too conservative; we like to sit here and let the stuff speak for itself. But I tell you, Fellow Old Timers, you can't do that nowadays. It's all right for a State to build up a Reputation for Modesty and be known as always having a good word to say for the other place, but I tell you we have carried it too far for our own good.

Of course I can appreciate you other old Timers' feelings in the matter. You have been here and helped build it to what it even is today, and you resent these Johnny Newcomers coming in and spoiling all of our old customs and Traditions. I know it is hard to change with the Times. We old Timers who have seen this place grow from what it was 2 and a half years ago to what it is today, must realize these stacks of young fellows coming in here the last two weeks must have the right idea, and we must begin to realize that after all it is the general welfare of the entire community we are after.

So, Fellow Members, if my little speech has been the means of changing just one of you from your Iron Clad rule of Modesty in regard to your Home state, why I will feel that my little efforts will not have been in vain.

So from now on I am for letting the World know of California, even if the rest of the State does disapprove of it, and I sit down amid HISSES from the MODEST Oldtimers.

PROMOTING THE OCEANLESS ONE PIECE SUIT

I WANT TO DO SOMETHING FOR THE HOME TOWN GIRL SO SHE CAN STAY AT HOME AND SHOW HOW AND WHAT SHE IS MADE OF.

PROMOTING THE OCEANLESS ONE PIECE SUIT

EVERYBODY at some time in life feels a call within Him or Her, as the gender may be, to try and Promote something or other, that is to form a Company and sell Stock. We have all bought so much and been stung so often that we want to try the side where the Money comes in, instead of going out.

One-third of the people in the United States promote, while the other two-thirds Provide. There are more commissions paid out to Stock Salesmen than are ever collected by Stock Buyers. So, after living honest for years, the thing naturally becomes monotonous and we feel a hankering to Promote.

Now, I had reached that stage in life where I had thought maybe I would get by clear to the end without Promoting something and sticking my Friends. But the old Bug has bit me; the old Make-it-easy-without-working has got me. So I am now branching out as a Promotor, Throwing the Rope, Chewing Gum, Acting a Fool in the Movies, Robbing Ziegfeld, and Writing for a Living. All these are side lines from now on. I am now a Promotor. A Promotor is a man who would rather stick a Friend than to sell Henry Ford a Synagogue.

Of course my proposition is different. (Did you ever hear one of them pull that Gag before?)

My proposition is of Interest to every Town of any size in America. I am forming Clubs, called Swimming or Bathing Clubs, or any Aquatic name. A great many Towns have been denied the privilege of having these Clubs, heretofore, as they were not siutated near any Body of Water. Now I have been to all the prominent Beaches in the East, and this summer have had a chance to study the various Water Resorts of California.

I have paid particular attention to the Habits and procedure of Club Members and their Guests and I think I can do the same for the Non-irrigated Portion of this Country as is being enjoyed by the Tidal Wave region.

I come into your Town and start promoting (we will call it a swimming or Beach Club). I sell memberships for, we will say, the nominal sum of 500 dollars a piece. That makes it high enough to keep out the substantial people who really after all are rather old-fashioned, and allows us to take into our Club some of our most prominent Bootleggers, Oil Magnates, who have worked their way up from the bottom in the last year, and just the people of the Town who do things—in other words, the ones who belong.

We build the Club House (a rather long rambling affair) on some ground which we can get at a nominal figure (as I will explain the value of Citizens like we will have being located in their midst, and what our Club will do for the surrounding Land). Now, the great advantage that my Clubs will have over the present ones in our Beach Cities is that we will build ours right in the heart of the Town, so the Tired Business Man can reach it even for Lunch, whereas in other places they have to go miles to reach a Beach Club. We will have a Uniformed man at the door to meet the Cars, as nothing impresses the newly rich so much as Gold Braid.

Our Cafe prices will be high enough so that if a Member takes a friend any other place he will be considered rather a short Sport. Each member will have his Private Locker (including a Corkscrew), where he can change to his bathing Suit. There will be a wide Veranda under awnings where

Members may dine in their Suits, and other Tables which are not protected from the Rays of the Sun, where the more Hardy Members may sit and acquire a Tan.

Of course one item of expense in connection with these Clubs which will require me to expend quite a tidy sum is having Ocean Sand transported to these Towns and then by Truck to the center of the City.

This sand must be spread very, very thick, as the principal pastime of the Members and Guests will be to lay right down in it and try and cover each other entirely up. Oh, it's a ripping experience that you in the inland Cities have missed, if you have never tried it.

Mind you, this 500 dollars which I receive per each will not all be profit as I will be called upon to purchase a Medicine Ball or so. That is a Beach Sport that only the most Athletic and reckless of our Membership would dare enter into—tossing this ferocious Ball from one to the other. I have seen a Game of it last, if there were Female Spectators, as long as three or four minutes.

Then, for the more skilled, there is Baseball on the Beach which is played with a Rubber Tennis

Ball. I have seen men graduate from that right into some of our best Tea and Cake Hounds.

We will have beautifully striped Umbrellas placed at intervals over the Beach for those who become fatigued in parading. When there is a big crowd and you have to walk by everybody in your Bathing Suit it tires one more than the uninitiated would think. And we'll have a Life Guard (perhaps a Native of Honolulu if we can procure one). At any rate, we will get the most sunburned one we can, for the less fortunate ones to compare their Tan with. He will be provided with Smelling Salts, and other restoratives in case a Wife should unexpectedly discover her own Husband with some other One Piece Suit Female Companion.

There will be Life Lines across the sands, so the more fore-sighted of the members can find their way during the afternoon back and forth to their Lockers.

Now, I think I have enumerated all that is required to successfully operate one of these Beach Clubs. Of course, most of them heretofore have had Water but in all my experience (which runs over a term of years) I have never seen a Member willfully enter this Water. Years ago at one of the Eastern Beaches they claim a man went into the water, but this has never been verified, and so far as the ladies go, there hasn't been a swell Bathing Suit wet since Kellermann retired.

Now you see my scheme. I have laid it before you. Nobody ever thought of it because they were not a close observer like I have been. They just naturally thought Water was required, but it is the most unnecessary thing connected with a Beach Club. Of course, Showers are provided for those who do not care to sleep with sand in their bed.

Just think of a Club right at your door where you can run down and change Clothes and display your figure without having to go to Palm Beach or Del Monte! Besides, I am showing you how you can display it to the People who you want to see it—not to a lot of strangers. Show it right where it will do you the most good.

If I had thought of this sooner and we had had one in my home of Claremore, Oklahoma (home of best Radium Water in the World) and I could have paraded up and down with my shape, I would have been able to settle down a lot earlier.

I tell you my scheme is a boost for home Talent. Many a Girl, if she could have shown off properly at home, would have never had to leave there. Now, if you think my scheme is crazy, you go to the Ocean where there is a Beach to parade on and see how many ever go in swimming where there is nothing but Swimming Water.

No sir, the Sand and the Clothes are the thing —not the Water. So I will put my scheme over, not only for the selfish motive of making money, but because I want to do something for the home Town Girl who hasn't the money to go to Narragansett Pier to be properly appreciated, but can stay at home and show how and what she is made of.

WARNING TO JOKERS: LAY OFF THE PRINCE

SO I GOT ME SOME OF THOSE LONG-HANDLED WOODEN HAMMERS AND STARTED IN AT POLO.

WARNING TO JOKERS: LAY OFF THE PRINCE

I WANT hereby, and hereon, to publicly issue a protest to my fellow Writers, and Comedians, against the use of Cartoons, Editorials, Paragraphs, Free Verse, or any form of Public Notice, Jibing, or Poking Fun or attempting to be Funny, at the Expense of the Prince of Wales, falling off his Horse.

My reasons are two fold, first on account of it being passé, and secondly on account of the happenings of the past week to my own Immediate Person. Now everything is funny as long as it is happening to somebody Else, but when it happens to you, why it seems to lose some of its Humor, and if it keeps on happening, why the entire laughter kinder Fades out of it.

Last year in New York it was one of my sure fire subjects to remark about the Prince of Wales staking himself out a six foot Claim in some part of England. And I remember one choice morsel of Gossip I had was that I was going to get appointed as Ambassador to England so I could go riding with the Prince and be able to rope his Horse and bring him Back to him. And another was, "I see where the Prince of Wales fell off his Horse again today. But that ain't News any more. If he stayed on That Would Be News." Well that always knocked the audience right back on their Flasks.

Now in those days, which was a Year ago, that was very Komical both to me and the audience. But of course now it has finally reached the Comic Strip Cartoons, really earlier than a joke generally does, and even the Editorial Writers are commenting on it, in what they term a lighter vein. Now an Editorial Writer is the last man in the World to find anything out, so you will see how old and out of date it must be to refer to now.

But all this has nothing to do with my real Reason. I always have a few old Ponies for me and the Children to play around with, so somebody said, "Will, why don't you play Polo? Anybody that can ride can play Polo." And me, like a Fool, believed him. Why that is as absurd as saying anybody that can walk would make a good Golf Player, or anybody that looks good in a Bathing Suit will make a good swimmer.

Now I want it distinctly understood that I did

not take up Polo for any Social Prestige, or to make myself pointed out as a Man about Town. If I was the Champion Polo Player of the World, I still couldn't drink a Cup of Tea without using the saucer. And another reason I always hesitated on taking up the Game was account of the White Breeches. I had always been reared to believe that White Breeches should be concealed beneath Black or Gray ones—at least in Public.

The people that think riding a Horse is all there is to Polo, are the same people that think Curls are all there is to Mary Pickford. I can also walk, but I can't sweep a Golf Ball into one of those Holes with a Broom.

So I got me some of those long handled wooden Hammers and started in at Polo. You know some men like to have their Fields harrowed and plowed, and I had not played Polo two days until I was offered a job to come over and Play on their Ground as they wanted it dug up. Finally I got so every once in a while I would hit the Ball. But it seemed like every time I hit the Ball it would get mad and go off in an opposite direction.

Well, finally I got to playing in Practice Games, more for the Comedy I would cause than through any good I might do my side. If the Purple and Whites had a Game I might wear a Purple Jersey, but in reality I would be playing with the Whites.

Then come a Polo Tournament held at Coronado Beach. So as I was scheduled to play in one of the Minor League, or Small Time events, I go down and one day we are having a Friendly practice Game with a few looking on. Three of us beginners all bump together, Mind you, we are all three on the same side. We knock our Horses down, I fall on my head and of course, am not hurt.

The Referee called an Unusual Foul. He said I had fouled by running over two of my own side. Well, the next day was the Big game; we were to play the 11th Cavalry from Monterey. They sure were a fine bunch of Boys, and hard Riders. Things were going along Pretty Good until along about the 3rd Act, I was on a new Pony who suddenly reared up and Fell Back on Me. There he was, a laying right across my Intermission. My Head was out on one side and my Feet on the other; that was all you could see. When he got up I knew for the first time how the Prince must have felt.

Well, everything goes K. O. for two more periods. I am on a Friend's Horse and coming lickerty split down the field, when for no Reason at all the horse crosses his front legs and starts turning Somersaults. They picked me up just south of Santa Barbara.

The crowd all said, "Oh that's Will Rogers the Comedian. He just does that for laughs." The Papers next day all said, "Comedian Spills off Horse Twice at Polo Game."

Now I will admit there was not quite the same Publicity given to all my various Falls as to those of the Prince. But the hurt was just as bad. Everybody that reads about it had been kidding me about being the Local Prince of Wales of America. But what I want to know from some of these Newspaper Riders is what I am supposed to do in case the Horse falls.

Are the Prince and I supposed to fall With the Horse, or are we supposed to stay up there in the air until he gets Up, and comes back up under us? Every fall that the Prince has had has been caused by a falling Horse, not by being thrown From one. In the future the Prince and I will personally pay in the papers for the extra two lines that will announce that "the Horse going down had something to do with our going off."

England is all worked up over his numerous Falls, but up to now no one has manifested much interest in any of mine, only for laughing purposes. At least none of the prominent Washington Politicians have asked me to cease my Riding. I want some concern paid to my welfare. In my falls I am not fortunate enough to spill any Royal Blood, but it's my Blood, and it's all I got. It's kinder funny but no matter how common our blood is, we hate to Lose any of it.

I saw a Picture in the Paper last summer where the Prince was on one of his Horses and its name was Will Rogers. Now I got all swelled Up when I saw he had a Horse named for me, but maybe that was the one that has been doing all this high and lofty Tumbling. As a suggestion, if our respective Countries want to do something to protect our Welfare, the best thing I can suggest would be to get us some Horses that can stand up, for the Prince and I both have to take every Precaution to protect our Looks. It would be terrible if his face was marred. And I certainly don't want anything to happen to Mine to make it look Better. My living depends on it, just as it Is.

The only thing that makes me sore is that I haven't got the nerve to do some of the riding stunts that the Prince goes after. He goes over Jumps that I wouldn't have the nerve to climb over on foot. Then if he gets a fall a lot of us alleged Humorists (who would be afraid to lead one of his horses to water with a 20 foot Halter rope) start in re-writing original Jokes about the Prince's Horsemanship.

I saw a Picture of one of his Falls, where the Horse had fallen trying for a Water Jump. Why that Jump was so wide, that I bet we haven't got a Joke Writer in this country could swim across it, and not over two could row over it.

I am not overly strong for Royalty, but if I had to have one of Them over me I don't know of one that I would rather have than this same Bird, and most of this Admiration has been won by his Horsemanship, not by the Lack of it.

Lots of women have it in for him because he has not married, But with all of them making a silly play for him, I admire his Judgment as much as his Horsemanship. So here is an appeal to my fellow Jokesters: If you want to kid somebody on their Riding go to Central Park, don't go to England unless, as I say, you have some Solution for a man staying up while the Horse is going Down.

P. S. I only had one thing to be thankful for in my falls. I practically Ruined the only Pair of White Breeches I had, of course, it's all right with the Prince—he can wear his Daddy's. But from now on I will get to play in Chaps.

SPRING IS HERE, WITH POEMS AND BATH TUBS

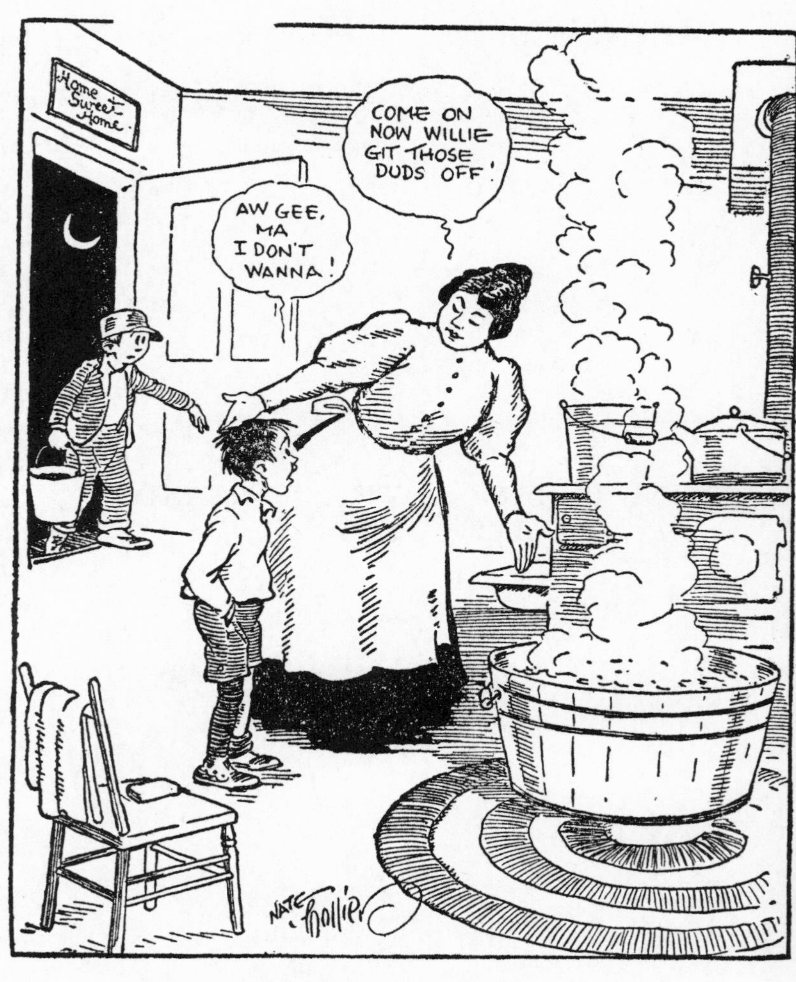

THE FAMILY WASH-TUB WAS DRAGGED UP BY THE FIRE.

SPRING IS HERE, WITH POEMS AND BATH TUBS

WELL, there has been quite a bit happened since I last communed with you. Spring is coming; I can tell by the Poetry and the Real Estate ads. A Poet exists all year just to get his Poem published in the Spring. Then when he sees it in print he starts getting next Spring's verse all ready. These early Spring Real Estate ads read, "This House is located on the shady banks of a Beautiful stream." Say, if there is a beautiful stream anywhere now the Rail Road runs along it and all you have to do is to get run over by a freight train to reach this beautiful stream.

A favorite ad is, "Beautiful Home in heart of the most exclusive Residential District, 5 Master Bedrooms and 9 baths; Owner going to Europe." Now let's just take that ad out and dissect it and see what it is.

In a Real Estate man's eye, the most exclusive part of the City is wherever he has a House to sell. The Dog Pound may be on one side and the City Incinerator on the other but it's still exclusive. And it is, too, for it will be the only house in the world so situated.

Five Master Bedrooms! Now, they get that Master junk from English ads where the man may be the master. Still, I don't know why they call all the rooms his. Over here they call them Master Bedrooms but the Wife will pick out the Poorest one for him, and keep the other 4 Good ones for Company.

Now, to the ordinary man on reading that Ad of 9 Baths, that would be an insult to his cleanliness. A Man would have to be awful Busy to support that many Baths, unless, of course, he neglected some of them. The ad might better have read, "Buy our home and live in a Bath Tub." The biggest part of City homes nowadays have more Baths than Beds. So, while they can't always ask their Company to stay all night as they have no place to put them, they can at least ask them to Bathe. So, when you are invited out now, you can always be assured of your private Bath, but you must leave before Bed-time.

When you visit a friend's newly finished Home you will be shown through all the Bath rooms, but when you leave you couldn't, to save your soul, tell where the dining room was. They seem to kinder want to camouflage or hide that nowadays. There is such little eating being done in the Homes now that a dining room is almost a lost art. Breakfast is being served in bed, Dinner at the Cabaret with dancing attached, and Lunch—no up-to-date Man would think of going anywhere but to his Clubs for lunch. Besides, didn't he hear a funny one and must get to the Club to bore his alleged friends with it? He will talk everybody's left ear off all day and come home and bite his Wife's off if she asks him to tell her the news.

And then they have such an enlightening custom nowadays. Every body of men who can think of a name have a Club. And is not Congressman Blindbridle, who has just returned from a free Government trip to Bermuda, going to deliver a Message at today's Luncheon on "Americanism, Or what we owe to the Flag?"

Now, as the dining room space has been eliminated to make room for an additional Bath, most of the eating, if one happens to be entertaining at home, is done Off The Lap. This custom of slow starvation has shown vast improvement of late. Instead of the Napkins being of Paper, why, they have been supplanted by almost-linen ones with beautiful hemstitching. That's to try and get your mind off the lack of nourishment. As I say, the Napkin is hand sewn but the Lettuce Sandwiches still come from the Delicatessen.

Why, in the good old days, they couldn't have fed you on your lap 'cause you couldn't have held all they would give you. Now you have to feel for it to find it.

But the Husband does come home some time during the Day or Night, for is not the overhead on his outlay of Baths going on all the time, and shouldn't he be getting home to get some good out of some of them?

It's not the high cost of Living that is driving us to the Poor House,—It's the high Cost of bathing. The big question today is not what are you going to pay for your plot of ground, but what kind of fixtures are you going to put in your legion of Bath Rooms. Manufacturers of Porcelain and Tile have Supplanted the Pocket Flask as our principal commodity.

The interest on unpaid-for Bath Rooms would pay our National Debt.

Now, mind you, I am not against this modern

accomplishment, or extravagance, of ours. I realize that these Manufacturers of Fixtures have advanced their Art to the point where they are practically modern Michael Angelos. Where, in the old days, an Elephant Hook was almost necessary for a Wife to drag her Husband toward anything that looked like Water, today those Interior Bath Decorators can almost make one of those things inviting enough to get in without flinching.

But, in doing so, they have destroyed an American Institution, and ruined the only Calendar that a Child ever had. That was the Saturday Night Bath. Nowadays a Child just grows up in ignorance. From the Cradle to the Altar he don't know what day of the week it is. In those good old days he knew that the next morning after that weekly Ear washing he was going to Sunday School. Now he has not only eliminated the Bath on Saturday but has practically eliminated the Sunday School, for neither he nor his Parents know when Sunday comes.

But, in those days, that old Kitchen Stove was kept hot after supper. And not only the Tea Kettle was filled but other Pots and Pans, and the Family Wash Tub was dragged up by the Fire, and you went out to the Well and helped your Pa draw some Water to mix with that hot. While you was doing that, your Ma, if you stayed Lucky and had a Ma up to then, was a getting out all the clean Clothes and a fixing the Buttons, and a laying out the schedule of who was to be first. And She was the only one could tell just how much hot Water to put in to make it right. And if anybody had to feel of the hot water and get burned it was always her, not you, and she found dirt behind, and in, your Ears that all the highfaluting Fixtures in the World can't find today.

Now that was an event. It meant something. It brought you closer together. But now bathing is so common there's No Kick To It. It's just *Bla!!*

The Romans started this Bath Gag; now look what become of them. They used to have the most beautiful Baths, kind of a Municipal Bath, where they all met and strolled around and draped themselves on Marble Slabs. It was a kinder Society event. It compared to our modern Receptions. I have seen some beautiful Paintings of them, but I have yet to see a Scene where a Roman was in the Water. But they did look, oh, just too cunning, sunning themselves out on the Concrete Banks of those Pools. It must have been like visiting our modern Beaches, where no one can swim but the Life Guard, and they don't know that he can as he has never been called on to go in. But, like the Romans, our Girls can arrange themselves in the most bewitching shapes out on the sand, which, after all, must be much more comfortable than the Asphalt that those little Cæsars had to spread themselves over.

I tell you if Baths keep on multiplying in the modern Home as they have lately it won't be 5 Years till a Bath Tub will be as necessary in a home as a Cocktail Shaker.

If two members of the same household have to use the same Bath, it is referred to now as a Community Tub.

Statistics have proven that there are 25 Bath Tubs sold to every Bible.

And fifty to every Dictionary, and 389 to every Encyclopedia.

Proving that, while we may be neglecting the Interior, we are looking after the exterior.

If the Father of our Country, George Washington, was Tutankhamened tomorrow, and, after being aroused from his Tomb, was told that the American People today spend two Billion Dollars yearly on Bathing Material, he would say, "WHAT GOT 'EM SO DIRTY?"

MR. FORD AND OTHER POLITICAL SELF-STARTERS

MR. FORD AND OTHER POLITICAL SELF-STARTERS

WELL, there has been quite a stir in the Political News. The big news was the Ford for President talk, made more important by Mr. Hearst announcing that he would back him if he run on an independent Ticket. It only shows you what both of the old line Parties are degenerating into. Nobody wants to associate with either one of them.

I think that it will be the biggest boost Mr. Ford will have that he don't belong to either Party. It's getting so if a man wants to stand well socially he can't afford to be seen with either the Democrats or the Republicans.

I expect, if it was left to a vote right now by all the people, Mr. Ford would be voted for by more people than any other man. But, if it come to a question of counting those votes, I doubt if he even run third. For, with all the mechanical improvements they have in the way of adding machines, and counting machines, they can't seem to invent anything to take the place of the old Political mode of counting—two for me and one for you.

More men have been elected between Sundown and Sunup, than ever were elected between Sunup and Sundown.

Our public men are speaking every day on something, but they ain't saying anything. But when Mr. Harding said that, in case of another war that capital would be drafted the same as men, he put over a thought that, if carried out, would do more to stop Wars than all the International Courts and Leagues of Nations in the World.

Of the three things to prevent wars, League of Nations, International Court, and this Drafting of Capital, this last one is so far ahead of the others there is no comparison. When that Wall Street Millionaire knows that you are not only going to come into his office and take his Secretary and Clerks but that you come in to get his Dough, say Boy, there wouldn't be any war. You will hear the question: "Yes, but how could you do it?"

Say, you take a Boy's life, don't you? When you take Boys away you take everything they have in the World, that is, their life. You send them to war and part of that life you don't use you let him come back with it. Perhaps you may use all of it. Well, that's the way to do with wealth. Take all he has, give him a bare living the same as you do the Soldier. Give him the same allowance as the Soldier—all of us that stay home. The Government should own everything we have, use what it needs to conduct the whole expenses of the war and give back what is left, if there is any, the same as you give back to the Boy what he has left.

There can be no Profiteering. The Government owns everything till the war is over. Every Man, Woman and Child, from Henry Ford and John D. down, get their Dollar and a Quarter a day the same as the Soldier. The only way a man could profiteer in war like that would be to raise more Children.

If any man went before the People on a platform of that kind and put it over, he could remain President till his Whiskers got so long he could make a fortune just picking the lost Golf Balls out of them. But, no, it will never get anywhere. The rich will say it ain't practical, and the poor will never get a chance to find out if it is or not.

Lincoln made a wonderful speech under similar conditions one time: "That this Nation under God, shall have a new Birth of Freedom, and that Government of the people, by the People, for the People, shall not perish from this earth."

Now, every time a Politician gets in a speech, he digs up this Gettysburg quotation. He recites it every Decoration day and practices the opposite the other 364 days.

If our Government is by the people, how is it the Candidate with the most votes by the people, going into a Presidential Convention never got nominated?

Now, Lincoln meant well, but he only succeeded in supplying an applause line for every Political Speaker who was stuck for a finish.

And that's the way with Mr. Harding; he certainly meant well, for I can imagine his feelings after having to mingle for the last 2 years with some of our War Millionaires who are hanging around Washington, just laying off between Wars.

And, in after Years, so will this speech of Mr. Harding's be quoted, but the minute the fellow gets through quoting it he will go sign a War Contract for Cost Plus 10 percent.

In our Decoration day speechmaking Mr. Taft spoke at some unveiling of a Monument in Cincinnati. He made an Alibi for the Supreme Court. I don't know what prompted him to tell the dead what the Court was doing, unless it was some man who had died of old age waiting for a decision from that August Body.

We can always depend on Judge Gary for a weekly laugh in his speeches. But lately he had the prize wheeze of his career. He had his accomplices make an investigation of the Steel Industry, and they turned in a report that it was much more beneficial to man to work 12 hours a day than 8. They made this report so alluring that it is apt to make people who read it decide to stay the extra 4 hours on their jobs, just through the Health and enjoyment they get out of it. I never knew Steel work was so easy till I read that report. Why, the advantages they enumerated in this report would almost make a Bootlegger trade jobs with a Steel Worker. But here is the kick. Judge Gary got up to read this report before the stock holders who had made it out. He read for one hour in favor of a 12 hour day. Then he was so exhausted they had to carry him out, and Charley Schwab had to go on reading the sheet.

Now, if the Judge couldn't work an hour, how did he expect his workers to do 12 every day?

After Schwab read for 2 hours the audience was carried out.

It was the greatest boost for the 12 hour day I ever heard of. I am thinking of going out there and working for them, but, if it is such a pleasure to work 12 hours, I am going to try and get them to let me work 18, at least, for I don't believe I would get enough pleasure out of just 12.

So if you don't hear of me next week, you will know I just enjoyed myself to death in Judge Gary's Steel Mills in Pittsburgh.

WILSON COULD LAUGH AT A JOKE ON HIMSELF

FINALLY A WARDEN KNOCKED AT MY DRESSING ROOM AND SAID: "YOU DIE IN
MORE MINUTES FOR KIDDING YOUR COUNTRY."

WILSON COULD LAUGH AT A JOKE ON HIMSELF

SOME of the most glowing and deserved tributes ever paid to the memory of an American have been paid to our past President Woodrow Wilson. They have been paid by learned men of this and all Nations, who knew what to say and how to express their feelings. They spoke of their close association and personal contact with him. Now I want to add my little mite even though it be of no importance.

I want to speak and tell of him as I knew him for he was my friend. We of the stage know that our audiences are our best friends, and he was the greatest Audience of any Public Man we ever had. I want to tell of him as I knew him across the footlights. A great many Actors and Professional people have appeared before him, on various occasions in wonderful high class endeavors. But I don't think that any person met him across the footlights in exactly the personal way that I did on five different occasions.

Every other Performer or Actor did before him

exactly what they had done before other audiences on the night previous, but I gave a great deal of time and thought to an Act for him, most of which would never be used again and had never been used before. Owing to the style of Act I used, my stuff depended a great deal on what had happened that particular day or week. It just seemed by an odd chance for me every time I played before President Wilson that on that particular day there had been something of great importance that he had just been dealing with. For you must remember that each day was a day of great stress with him. He had no easy days. So when I could go into a Theatre and get laughs out of our President by poking fun at some turn in our National affairs, I don't mind telling you it was the happiest moments of my entire career on the stage.

The first time I shall never forget, for it was the most impressive and for me the most nervous one of them all. The Friars Club of New York one of the biggest Theatrical Social Clubs in New York had decided to make a whirlwind Tour of the principal Cities of the East all in one week. We played a different City every night. We made a one night stand out of Chicago and New York.

We were billed for Baltimore but not for Washington. President Wilson came over from Washington to see the performance. It was the first time in Theatrical History that the President of the United States came over to Baltimore just to see a Comedy.

It was just at the time we were having our little Set Too, with Mexico, and when we were at the height of our Note Exchanging career with Germany and Austria. The house was packed with the Elite of Baltimore.

The Show was going great. It was a collection of clever Skits, written mostly by our stage's greatest Man, George M. Cohan, and even down to the minor bits was played by Stars with big Reputations. I was the least known member of the entire Aggregation, doing my little specialty with a Rope and telling Jokes on National affairs, just a very ordinary little Vaudeville act by chance sandwiched in among this great array.

I was on late, and as the show went along I would walk out of the Stage door and out on the Street and try to kill the time and nervousness until it was time to dress and go on. I had never told Jokes even to a President, much less about one, especially to his face. Well, I am not kidding you when I tell you that I was scared to death. I am always nervous. I never saw an Audience that I ever faced with any confidence. For no man can ever tell how a given Audience will ever take anything.

But here I was, nothing but a very ordinary Oklahoma Cowpuncher who had learned to spin a Rope a little and who had learned to read the Daily Papers a little, going out before the Aristocracy of Baltimore, and the President of the United States, and kid about some of the Policies with which he was shaping the Destinies of Nations.

How was I to know but what the audience would rise up in mass and resent it? I had never heard, and I don't think any one else had ever heard of a President being joked personally in a Public Theatre about the Policies of his administration.

The nearer the time come the worse scared I got, George Cohan, and Willie Collier, and others, knowing how I felt, would pat me on the back and tell me, "Why he is just a Human Being; go on out and do your stuff". Well if somebody had come through the dressing room and hollered "Train for

Claremore Oklahoma leaving at once", I would have been on it. This may sound strange but any who have had the experience know, that a Presidential appearance in a Theatre, especially outside Washington, D. C. is a very Rare and unique feeling even to the Audience. They are keyed up almost as much as the Actors.

At the time of his entrance into the House, everybody stood up, and there were Plain Clothes men all over the place, back stage and behind his Box. How was I to know but what one of them might not take a shot at me if I said anything about him personally?

Finally a Warden knocked at my dressing room door and said, "You die in 5 more minutes for kidding your Country". They just literally shoved me out on the Stage.

Now, by a stroke of what I call good fortune, (for I will keep them always) I have a copy of the entire Acts that I did for President Wilson on the Five times I worked for him. My first remark in Baltimore was, "I am kinder nervous here tonight." Now that is not an especially bright remark, and I don't hope to go down in History on the strength of it, but it was so apparent to the audience that I was speaking the truth that they laughed heartily at it. After all, we all love honesty.

Then I said, "I shouldn't be nervous, for this is really my second Presidential appearance. The first time was when Bryan spoke in our town once, and I was to follow his speech and do my little Roping Act." Well, I heard them laughing, so I took a sly glance at the President's Box and sure enough he was laughing just as big as any one. So I went on, "As I say, I was to follow him, but he spoke so long that it was so dark when he finished, they couldn't see my Roping." That went over great, so I said "I wonder what ever become of him." That was all right, it got over, but still I had made no direct reference to the President.

Now Pershing was in Mexico at the time, and there was a lot in the Papers for and against the invasion. I said "I see where they have captured Villa. Yes, they got him in the morning Editions and the Afternoon ones let him get away." Now everybody in the house before they would laugh looked at the President, to see how he was going to take it. Well, he started laughing and they all followed suit.

"Villa raided Columbus New Mexico. We had a man on guard that night at the Post. But to show you how crooked this Villa is, he sneaked up on the opposite side." "We chased him over the line 5 miles, but run into a lot of Government Red Tape and had to come back." "There is some talk of getting a Machine Gun if we can borrow one. The one we have now they are using to train our Army with in Plattsburg. If we go to war we will just about have to go to the trouble of getting another Gun."

Now, mind you, he was being criticized on all sides for lack of preparedness, yet he sat there and led that entire audience in laughing at the ones on himself.

At that time there was talk of forming an Army of 2 hundred thousand men, so I said, "we are going to have an Army of 2 hundred thousand men. Mr. Ford makes 3 hundred thousand Cars every year. I think, Mr. President, we ought to at least have a Man to every Car." "See where they got Villa hemmed in between the Atlantic and Pacific. Now all we got to do is to stop up both ends." "Pershing located him at a Town called, Los Quas Ka Jasbo. Now all we have to do is to locate Los Quas Ka Jasbo." "I see by a headline that Villa escapes Net and Flees. We will never catch him then. Any Mexican that can escape Fleas is beyond catching." "But we are doing better toward preparedness now, as one of my Senators from Oklahoma has sent home a double portion of Garden Seed."

After various other ones on Mexico I started in on European affairs which at that time was long before we entered the war. "We are facing another Crisis tonight, but our President here has had so many of them lately that he can just lay right down and sleep beside one of those things."

Then I first pulled the one which I am proud to say he afterwards repeated to various friends as the best one told on him during the War. I said, "President Wilson is getting along fine now to what he was a few months ago. Do you realize, People, that at one time in our negotiations with Germany that he was 5 Notes behind?"

How he did laugh at that! Well, due to him being a good fellow and setting a real example, I had the proudest and most successful night I ever had on the stage. I had lots of Gags on other subjects but the ones on him were the heartiest laughs with him, and so it was on all the other occasions I played for him. He come back Stage at intermission and chatted and shook hands with all.

Some time I would like to tell of things he laughed at during the most serious stages of the Great War. Just think there were hundreds of millions of Human Beings interested directly in that terrible War, and yet out of all of them he stands, 5 years after it's over, as the greatest man connected with it. What he stood for and died for, will be strived after for years.

But it will take time for with all our advancement and boasted Civilization, it's hard to stamp out selfishness and Greed. For after all, Nations are nothing but Individuals, and you can't stop even Brothers from fighting sometimes. But he helped it along a lot. And what a wonderful cause to have laid down your life for! The World lost a Friend. The Theatre lost its greatest supporter. And I lost the most distinguished Person who ever laughed at my little nonsensical jokes. I looked forward to it every year. Now I have only to look back on it as my greatest memory.

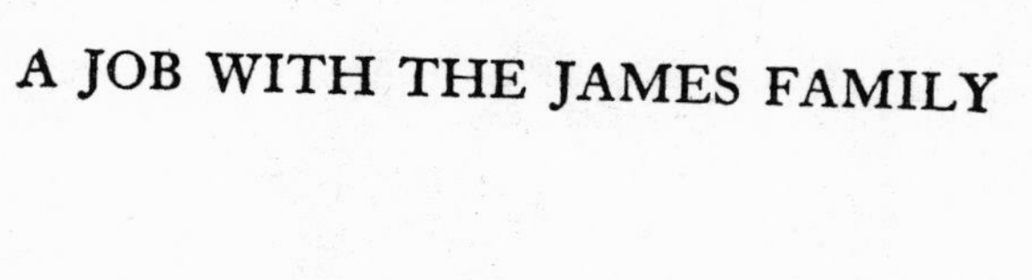

A JOB WITH THE JAMES FAMILY

I COULD JUST SORTER NONCHALANTLY STEP ON THE BRIDE'S TRAIN.

A JOB WITH THE JAMES FAMILY

Mr. Warren Gamaliel Harding.
President of these United States and
Viceroy of the District of Columbia.
Chevy Chase Golf Club, Washington, D. C.

My dear Mr. President,

I see where Mr. Harvey (I mean Col. or, rather, Ambassador) Harvey is coming back here again. Now I don't know if it's a slumming trip or just what it is, as he was here a few days ago. Maybe he forgot something in one of his Speeches and is coming back for an Encore. But in a later Paper I see where he is talking of resigning and not going back. Now, if that is the case, I hereby make this an open letter to you, Mr. President, as an application to take said Mr. Harvey (I mean Editor) Harvey's place.

I can tell by observation that it does not come under the Civil Service or competitive examination. Neither, on the other hand, is it a purely Political appointment, as Mr. Harvey adapted his Politics to fit the occasion. Now that would not be even necessary in my case as I have no Politics. I am for the Party that is out of Power, no matter which one it is. But I will give you my word that, in case of my appointment, I will not be a Republican; I will do my best to pull with you, and not embarrass you. In fact, my views on European affairs are so in accord with You, Mr. President, that I might almost be suspected of being a Democrat.

Now I want to enumerate a few of my qualifications for the position of Ambassador to the Court of James (I don't know whether it's St. or Jesse). But, anyway, it's some of the James Family.

My principal qualification would be my experience in Speechmaking. That, as statistics have proven, is 90 percent of the duties of a Diplomat. Now I can't make as many speeches as my predecessor, unless, of course, I trained for it. But I would figure on making up in quality any shortcomings I might have in endurance. For you know, Mr. President, there is no Race or People in the world who appreciate quality as the English do.

Now, the way I figure it out, what one has to do is to make his speeches so that they will sound one way to the English, and the direct opposite to the Hearst readers back over here. Now George (I don't mean King; I mean Col.) was rather unfortunate in that respect; he made them so they would sound two ways, but both Nations took the wrong way.

Now, for instance, if I wanted Mr. Balfour to take something back, I would just kid him into it; make him believe I didn't care whether he took it back or not. You know how it is, just like the Democrat Senators do with Lodge.

Another qualification that must not by any means be underestimated is my Moving Picture experience. You see, for an official position nowadays, we must pay more attention to how our public men screen if we are to have to look at them every day in the news films. We must not only get men with screen personality, but we must get men who know Camera angles and know when they are getting the worst of it in a picture and not be caught in the background during the taking of some big event.

Europeans are far ahead of us in this line of Diplomacy, and, if you don't watch them, you are liable to be found photographed with the Mob instead of the Principals. The thing is to do some little thing during the taking of the picture that will draw the audience's attention to you. For instance, during some Court ceremony, I could just playfully kick the King. Now you don't know how a little thing like that would get over with the public. Or, at one of the big weddings in the Abbey, I could just sorter nonchalantly step on the bride's train, as they passed by, perhaps ripping it off, or any little Diplomatic move like that. You don't realize how just little bits like that would make our Ambassador stand out over all the other Countries.

We have had an example of screen training right here at home. Take Josephus Daniels when he was working. We spent 4 years sitting in Picture Houses watching him launch Ships, and at every launching he could place himself at such an angle that you not only could not see the Democratic Governor's Daughter who was to break the Ginger Ale, but you couldn't even see the Ship. Now that was not accidental; that was Art.

And did you ever notice in the weekly News pictures how some Senators can take a chew of Tobacco right in the scene and you catch yourself watching them and no one else? Now those are just a few of the little things that we have to look after if we want to hold our own as the greatest Credit Nation north of Mexico.

Now, another thing, I ride horseback, so the Prince of Wales and I could ride together and, on account of my experience with the rope, I could catch his horse for him.

Then I play a little Polo, just enough to get hit in the mouth, but the English would enjoy that. When they heard the American Ambassador had got hit in the mouth and would have to cancel his speech at the Pilgrims Club, why, that would of course be good news to everybody. You see you have to give as well as receive in the Diplomatic Circles.

Now, to offset the above mentioned qualifications, I may lack a few Social ones, but what I lacked in knowledge I could make up in tact. I would not at any dinner pick up a single weapon until I saw what the Hostess was going to operate with first. When in doubt, tell a funny story till you see what the other fellow is going to do.

Then, of course, any glaring error on my part would be laid onto the customs of my Country and not on me personally.

Then I have an economy measure to recommend me. The Government is putting into commission the Leviathan, our biggest Ship, and I could, by entertaining on the Boat going over, save passage fee. I could arrange a Monologue on, "The Benefits and Accomplishments of Prohibition," and, as we passed the three mile limit, I could start in delivering it and perhaps relieve, or rather add to, the dryness of the trip. We would have to explain this to the Farmers of the country so they would not think the ship was getting this feature for nothing. It could not be considered as Ship Subsidy.

Now the feature that I feel rather modest about referring to, but which is really my principal asset, is my being able to wear Silk Knee Breeches—not only wear them, but what I mean, look like something in them.

It seems that the Lord instead of distributing my very few good points around as he does on most homely men, why, he just placed all of mine from the knee down. Now that this thing has come over there, it almost seems like I was inspired for the part. Say, I can put on those silk Rompers and clean up. Now I don't like to grab off a Guy's job by knocking him, but you know we haven't had a decent looking leg over there in years. Now Harvey's! Oh, but what's the use of arguing? You know you can't stay in the Follies 7 years on nothing. Well, it wasn't my good looks. So what was it but my Shape?

That brings us down to Golf. Now I will have to admit that my political education has been sadly neglected as I have never walked over many green pastures. Horses are too cheap for a man to spend half his life walking over the country looking for holes in the ground. But as I understand this lack of Golf will not handicap me in England as it would over here, as Mr. Volstead has not percolated into that land and the game is still fought out at the 19th hole. And, if I do say it myself, I do talk a corking Game of Golf. Then another thing, in looking over the results of the last two International Golf Tournaments I don't think they play the game there at all.

Now, Mr. President, if this suggestion receives the consideration that I think it deserves, I should like to get the appointment at once, as I want to get over there before all the king's Children are married. If one can't attend a royal marriage, why, their ambassadorship has been a failure as far as publicity is concerned for that event is the World's Series of England.

Now, if you can't send me there, don't, just because I have criticized some of the feminine members of official life in Washington, don't, for the Lord's sake, send me to Chile or Honduras or some of the outlandish places. I will even promise to hush rather than that.

Now, as to Salary, I will do just the same as the rest of the Politicians—accept a small salary as pin Money, AND TAKE A CHANCE ON WHAT I CAN GET.

Awaiting an early reply, I remain

Yours faithfully,

WILL ROGERS.

P.S. If you don't want me, Turkey wants me to represent them in Washington. So where would you rather have me—in England or Washington?

LET'S TREAT OUR PRESIDENTS LIKE HUMAN BEINGS

LET'S TREAT OUR PRESIDENTS LIKE HUMAN BEINGS

AS I am writing this away out here in California days before you read it, it's Sunday and everybody's thoughts and sympathies are with a train rushing clear across our Country, passing sorrowfully through little Towns with Just Folks standing bareheaded paying their respects to Just Folks going back to Marion to stay with Just Folks.

He goes to his resting place a Martyr, a martyr to the Boneheadedness of Reception Committees. You wouldn't ask your hired man to do in one week the amount of real physical work that each Committee asked him to do on one day. Imagine three long Speeches in one day in Seattle at different places, and Parade for two hours in the hot Sun with his hat off most of the time, besides a thousand other things he was asked to do.

Just suppose for instance you had a Guest coming to visit you. Would you start in having him entertain the Neighbors the minute he got in the House, and then keep every minute of his time occupied till train time, and then turn him over to the next bunch?

Why, no, you wouldn't think of such a thing. The first thing you think of when a friend comes from a long Journey is to have him rest, but because it is your President he don't need any. So when the next Congress meets they should pass a law to shoot all Reception Committees, or teach them consideration for other People.

If Jack Dempsey had left Washington and undertaken this same strain, when he got back Uncle Joe Cannon could have licked him.

Any of you who have slept, or tried to, on a Train at Night and got into a Town early in the morning, you know you don't feel like speaking or Parading. You want to go to a Hotel and go to bed. Now can you imagine the President's case? Every morning at 6 A. M. to be awakened by a Band (it wouldn't be so bad if it was a good Band) and you look out and there is the Town's best Citizens in Antique Hats, ready to show you the Fire House, the new Aqueduct, the High School, and City Hall. The smell of the Moth Balls from the long tail Coats of the Committee morning after morning, would give a man some kind of disease.

Now, every man on that Committee was nearly tired out at night and took a vacation the next day, but the President must go right on the same thing the next day, only worse, for every Town was trying to outdo the other. It's not only a hardship on the People you are entertaining but hard on everybody participating.

One Town will have a Flag composed of 5 thousand children, assembled and standing in the Hot sun for hours, not only spoiling their whole day but subjecting them to every known contagious disease. The next Town to be original will get 10 thousand Children to make up their Flag, and Make Their Parade 10 Miles as the Last One Only Paraded 5, even if they have to exhaust their Guest to do it.

Then, of course, he is always asked to speak out in the open. They have 60 acre Fields and put seats around them and call 'em Stadiums, and expect a man to talk in them. Anyone who has ever spoken outdoors knows what outdoor speaking does to your voice. The Town with the cheapest land and most Concrete can have the largest Stadium.

I have always claimed that Parades should be classed as a Nuisance and participants should be subject to a term in prison. They stop more work, inconvenience more People, stop more traffic, cause more accidents, entail more expense, and commit and cause I don't remember the other hundred misdemeanors. And what good are they? Half of them going along you don't know who they are, or what they are for. Even the People in them hate 'em. The most popular joke I had after the War in New York when the Boys were coming back and parading every day was, "If we really wanted to honor our Boys, why didn't we let them sit on the reviewing stands and make the people march those 15 miles?" They didn't want to parade, they wanted to go home and rest. But they wouldn't discharge a Soldier as long as they could find a new Street in a Town that he hadn't marched down, yet.

Of course, keep Circus Parades, for they really give enjoyment not only to kids but us old ones, too. As a remedy for this parading I would suggest that each Town set aside one Street, away out where there is nothing to interfere and give them that as Parade Street; then when some fellow or gang wants to try out a new Uniform or honor somebody, why let them parade up and down there just as long as they want to. If you think Parading is popular just see how many would go over there to see it. Parades nowadays think they are drawing a crowd when it's only people trying to get across the street to their business, not to see you Parade at all. So just set them aside a Street—that will stop it. The minute a Parader sees that no one is watching him he will stop and in that way you will eliminate all Parades.

I was on the Reception Committee of the Movie Industry that was to have met the President here in Los Angeles. Well, just as an example of what I said about the others, they decided that it might be showing partiality if they took him to any one Studio, so they decided to take him to all of them. In that way they could take up his entire time. Now, no one knew whether he wanted to go to any of them or not; we were deciding for him. Can you imagine being a Guest of the City of Carnegie, Pa., and the Committee showing you through all the Steel mills in Town?

Now, President Harding was quite an admirer of the Movies so I imagine he liked sausage, too. But Chicago didn't rush him off to the Packing Houses the minute he got there, to see it made.

According to his itinerary here, he was allowed 15 minutes to call on an Aunt whom he hadn't seen in years that lived here. That was to be his only relaxation while here. We were waiting to see how long Frisco's Parade would run so we could run ours longer.

Now, as just an example of the trip, he loved Golf (and as the later sad events have proven) it was good for him; it was the very Recreation needed. But do you think these Committees let him do it? No Sir, he only got out three times on the entire trip. I offered a suggestion here when they were making the arrangements, but like everything coming from a Comedian it was considered not practical. I wanted to let the Reception Committee go ahead and rent the Suits and be at the Station looking Funny just like these others he was used to day after day, but instead of dragging him off where he didn't know where he was going, why just say, "Mr. President, we have engaged a room at the Central Hotel. Here's a Ford Car at your disposal. Here's a Card to any Golf Course in our Town. Now we know you are tired, so you just make yourself at home these few days; do just as you please, we have no plans for you at all."

Well, my plan wasn't adopted; it was too late. But if it had been even partly tried in all the Towns on this trip we would have all been happy and had him with us today. The first Town that ever does do that with their visiting Guests and treat them as if Human, they will soon be wondering where all their popularity comes from.

You may have read in the Papers last year that the Diplomatic Relations were strained between President Harding and some of my Jokes on the Administration. Now, I want to say that nothing was farther from the truth. That was simply newspaper stuff. It was reported that he couldn't stand Jokes about the Administration. Why, he had a great sense of Humor and could stand all the jokes ever told about him or his Policies. The first time I met him Will Hays introduced me to him in the White House and he repeated to me a lot of jokes that I had told away before.

And I told him then: "Now Mr. Harding, I don't want you to think I am hard on you—all. You know I told some pretty hard ones on the Democrats when they were in; in fact I think I told funnier ones on the Democrats, as they were doing funnier things." I explained to him that it would not be fair to the Democrats to kid them while they were down, but the minute they get their head above Water again I will take a whack at them.

I met Will Hays just before I left New York in

June and he said, "Will, I had lunch with the President last week and he had me tell him all your new stuff on the Administration."

No, I don't think I ever hurt any man's feelings by my little gags. I know I never wilfully did it. When I have to do that to make a living I will quit. I may not have always said just what they would have liked me to say but they knew it was meant in good nature.

I never go to Detroit that I don't spend an entire day out with Henry Ford and I don't suppose there is a man living (barring the owners) that have told any more jokes on him than I have.

I liked President Harding. You see I had met him, and I don't believe any man could meet him and talk to him and not like him. Why, I said after first meeting him, "I thought I would be scared when they took me in but he made me feel just like talking to some good old prosperous Ranchman out home." That's why I can understand him wanting to meet as many people personally as possible, for to meet him meant another friend.

I only hope our Future Presidents can be gifted with his Sense of Humor and Justice.

He was a mighty good friend to us Theatrical

People; he was a good friend to ALL kinds of People.

For he had the right dope after all. Everybody is JUST FOLKS.

HE WAS A REAL HONEST-TO-GOD-MAN.

WHAT WITH FRUIT JUICE AND CON-
SOMME, IT WAS A WILD PARTY

IF MR. FORD HAD BEEN ELECTED WE WOULD HAVE BEEN THE MOUTHPIECE O[F]
THE ADMINISTRATION.

WHAT WITH FRUIT JUICE AND CONSOMME, IT WAS A WILD PARTY

THE Illiterate Digest is a weekly publication, devoted to straight reading matter. We have no picture section and I doubt if we will appeal to over 1%, of the Public as the success of a Publication is based nowadays on the amount of Pictures and Advertising that they have in them. Of course, all our news comes by Radio. But The Digest is a tried and operating Paper. In fact we are old timers in the field. This is our 4th issue and we have just bought out and combined The Weekly Blowout, a paper that was sponsoring Mr. Ford's Detour to the White House. After his famous announcement that 90 per cent of the People in this Country were satisfied, why, The Blowout couldn't withstand such untruth. Had Mr. Ford gone through and been elected why The Blowout would have become the mouthpiece of the Administration. So, while not crowing over the misfortune of a Competitor, we were able to procure the Title of said Paper as soon as it had lost the chances of getting our Government run as Mr. Ford would have run it on a "Tighten a Bolt as it Goes By" system. Now The Digest and Blowout combined, is looking for some other likely Candidate to boost. We have even got down to such sore straits that a Populist would not be overlooked.

The Digest has some real inside Hollywood dirt to dish up to you. For fear some competitor will get in and publish it first I will tell just what happened at a Wild Party that was given tonight at the home of the Editor of this very Gem of Truth. And what makes it worse the head of our Industry that was hired and supposed to keep the Scandal from our doorsteps, was the main Guest, Will Hays (the only man in the history of Industry that was ever hired for a job without him or the People that hired him knowing what he was hired for, yet still made so good they couldn't replace him). Will Hays, the man who made Harding President, and the Movies (partly) behave.

Well my Wife and I, aided and encouraged by Daughter Mary decided to put on a Wild Party. Hollywood had been getting all the Publicity and selling all the Real Estate through their Scandal, and here was Beverly Hills who could put it on just as Wild as they could, and we couldn't seem to get anywhere. So we looked around to find some Guest that would be well enough known, so that when we carried him home he would be recognized.

We thought of Will Hays. So about 6.30 P. M. who should come staggering in from across the street from the Hotel but our Guest. His brother was to have come with him, but the Brother is a Lawyer from Sullivan, Indiana, and not having had the experience and capacity of Will he had gone completely out earlier in the evening while being entertained by The Womans' Federation of Churches.

Well, Will was so loaded that he had on a dress suit. It was the first one that had ever been in our House, so Bill Jr. and Jim, who had just come in from Public School and refilled their Flasks commenced to laugh at the Suit, and we put a sheet over the Chairs so that he wouldn't get it dirty.

But by this time he was feeling so good he didn't care anyway, for the Industry had bought it for him—and about this time another Guest who lives right near fell into the door before we knew it. That was Miss Pauline Frederick.

She was all primed for a real old prolonged Rough House. She had brought the stuff along with her. She had under her arm a big bag of knitting. She was knitting a Blanket for one of my Polo Ponies. So we all staggered around there till one of the children thought of introducing Miss Frederick and Will.

Then, to make the Party real devilish I was to go and get another man's wife while he was away at work. She lived next door, so I sneaked out while my Wife wasn't looking and dashed right into the home of the young Mrs. Cornelius Vanderbilt Jrs. She slipped on something and we both complimented each other on account of her Husband having to be at the office getting out his Newspaper. She asked if the Party was to be so wild that she should take her Gun. I said, "Sure, let's do it right." So we blew back just as they are ready to get real wild and start eating.

By this time Jim and Bill are becoming reconciled to Hays' suit and start playing Baseball in the House. Hollywood can't put on anything wilder than that. Hays by this time is feeling so good he is telling a story complimenting a Democrat.

We all start off with a Fruit Cocktail and everybody commenced to loosen up and tell their right Salaries. Then comes some Consomme and I can tell you this old mixing of drinks is getting in its work. Daughter Mary started doing a Wild dance in the Living Room until Jim laid her out with a Baseball Bat. Then Hays got to telling what his Boy could do, and the party just went from one Debauch into another.

Will told us of his trip to England with Ambassador Harvey. He said he went for pleasure, and I tried to get him to really tell what he went for. I think it was to get the Prince of Wales to come out for Coolidge.

Between drinks of Broiled Chicken I tried to find out if he was going to be the Campaign Manager for Mr. Coolidge. But he seemed to think it was such a sure fire thing, that they would waste some less expensive man. I kinder sobered up for a minute and asked him what he thought they would do in this investigation into the Tea Pot Dome Oil Lease. He said he didn't think they could show where Sinclair ever gave Sectry Fall anything. He knew Sinclair was too smooth a giver for that.

I asked him what he thinks of us sending Warships to Mexico. So he tells me what a hard time they had getting down there. Washington wired to the nearest one to go down and it runs on the rocks before they got through reading the telegram. You know our Navigators now depend on Radio to tell them where they are.

The Navy hasn't had a Compass in three years. They start on a trip and the radio operator tunes in and gets Paul Whiteman's Orchestra playing somewhere, and when he comes to he is in a lifeboat. Bedtime stories have put 9 ships to sleep.

Then I asked him who we were going to protect down there, he said, why the Oil Men. I asked him who protects the Mexican Sheep Herder in this Country if somebody interferes with his Industry, and if Mexico had a Navy could she send it up here to protect him. He said No. So the moral of this is, Be an Oil Man not a Sheep Herder, and be sure to be born in a Country that has a Navy.

By this time we are all so full we have to leave the table, and the noise of moving chairs is something deafening.

It's now eight thirty and the neighbors can see the light in our house and begin to phone in about it to the Police. Miss Fredericks' Yarn runs out, and she begins to yawn. Jim, Mary and Bill being younger and less unaccustomed to the revelry, had to be literally carried to their beds. Scandal was running rampant, while my wife was getting them off. That left Bill and I with the two Women. I says, "What will we do, Bill," and he says, "Oh, I am in for anything." So I just up and said, "Let's go down to the barn and look at the Horses." So out we staggered at 9 o'clock in the night in the heart of Beverly Hills. Bill Hays, a man that is a leader in the Presbyterian Church—but it only shows you when this old Movie Spirit gets in you, you will do anything.

I lasso four or five horses and bring them out and show them to Bill, but he is all excited talking to the Ladies. They wanted to take a ride, but I didn't want to carry this thing too far. So we go back to the house and I finally get them into their Coats and Hats and walk them home.

My Wife and I we figure the walk will do them good. So when we come back and get in the house why it's actually 9:15.

So I hope by the aid of Bill to put old Beverley Hills on the map as a Wild Town. Bill says to me, "Will, if the Woman's Club ever finds this out they will stop your pictures". I says "That's a good joke on the Woman's Club, my Pictures have never started."

I know all the papers will have this so I just want to beat them to it.

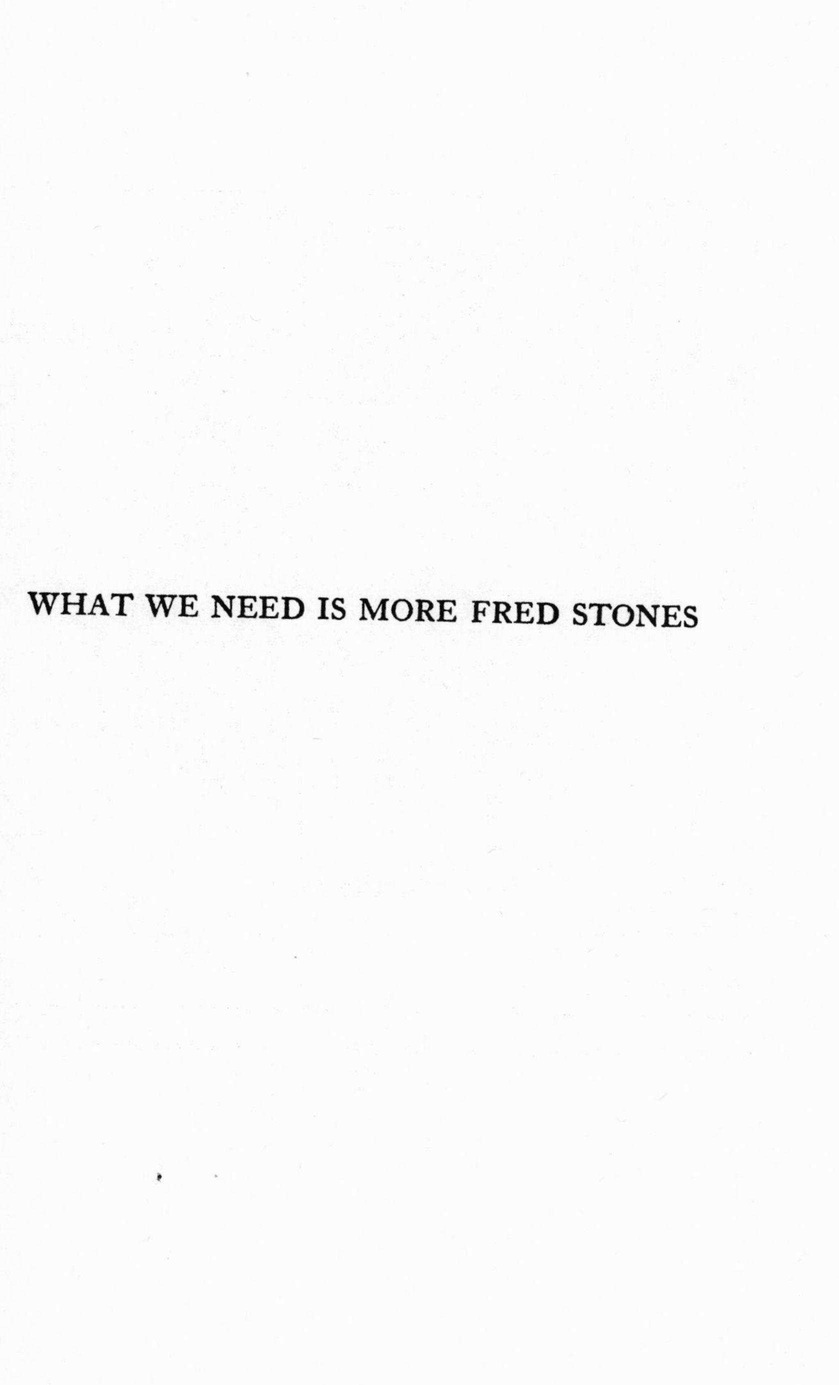

WHAT WE NEED IS MORE FRED STONES

HE STARTED AT FOUR OR FIVE YEARS OF AGE AND HAS WORKED ON NEW STUNTS EVERY DAY OF HIS LIFE.

WHAT WE NEED IS MORE FRED STONES

NOW I am not going to tell you any jokes today as jokes are not good for you to read every day. You will have to look to the Washington dispatches from Congress for your humor.

A Comedian is not supposed to be serious nor to know much. As long as he is silly enough to get laughs, why, people let it go at that. But I claim you have to have a serious streak in you or you can't see the funny side in the other fellow. Last Sunday night a Young Girl who had made a big hit in the Salvation Army preaching on the Street in New York, decided to go out and give religious Lectures of her own. So on her first appearance I was asked by her to introduce her. She said she would rather have me than a Preacher, or a Politician, or any one else. Well, I could understand being picked in preference to a Politician, as that is one Class us Comedians have it on for public respect, but to be chosen in preference to a Preacher was something new and novel.

The meeting was held in a Theatre, as you have

to fool some New Yorkers to get them in to hear a Sermon. Well, it took no great stretch of imagination to say something good for the Salvation Army, which, by the way, lots of People think was made by the late war. Why, the Salvation Army was just as great 10 years ago as it is today—not so big, but just as great. Ask any down-and-out fellow and he will tell you he knew of the good of the Salvation Army long before he ever heard there was a Kaiser.

Well, it seems like a Coincidence that, as I was trying to say something in a serious way for the first time before a New York Audience, why, away out in Butte, Montana, the best friend I have was going up to a Minister with a Bible in his hand and asking him if he didn't think "the Lord would recognize a Comedian."

So that is why you will get this Story and no jokes today.

Now a great many people, knowing my regard and friendship for Fred Stone, asked me if I was surprised. No, I was not. It was the shortest jump, from his life to a religious one, that any man ever made.

But it was a BIG thing to do, and I am certainly

pleased that he did it, for it will have a tremendous influence for good, not only on the people of our profession but on every one who reads about it. When you consider that the biggest and highest salaried and busiest Man we have in our profession can stop and give some of his time to religion, it is a lesson to the rest of us. Now, it has been my good fortune to have been very close friends with Fred for years. I have lived in his home and spend all my spare time there while playing in New York. We Rope and Ride and play together all the time. He has two wonderful homes on Long Island, one all fixed up like a Western Ranch with lots of Horses and a Polo field of his own on his place.

Then I am asked why he did this do I suppose. He did it because from childhood he had been raised up by the Dearest old Mother and Father you ever saw. That Christian teaching which she put into his head as a little Kid, when he started out doing a Tight Rope walking act in a little Circus, is just coming out. He was brought up to do right and never knew anything else. Just to watch him with his Mother and Father today you will understand he didn't have to go far to see a Preacher.

Then he has the most ideal home life. His every

thought is for his Family. His Wife is of the profession, and I have often heard my Wife say that Mrs. Stone is the most wonderful and devoted Mother she ever saw (and Women have a way of knowing those things).

And three lovely Daughters, the oldest, Dorothy, 18, who is with him in his show and is as talented as her Father and Mother. And so are the others. All are being trained for a Stage career. So you see he don't think so bad of the Stage.

He is the best loved Actor on the Stage today. He plays to the highest type audience of any Musical Show. He is the only Musical comedy comedian that has Matinees packed with Children, for none of our other Musical Comedy Comedians has ever been able to please the Children and the grown ups too. He is as great a Pantomimist on the stage as Chaplin is on the screen.

Now, people must not get the idea that this is a remote case in our Business. It is, of course, on account of the prominence of the man that we have heard so much of it, and if he had known that it would be broadcasted in this way it would have been the only thing to make him hesitate. No one can say that Fred Stone was ever a publicity seeker. He is too sincere in all he does for that. I think if all Churches in communities where Theatrical people live were canvassed you would find there are as many of them in attendance as any other line of people. And when you come to Charity and trying to help some one who is in need, you will find them, not only holding their own, but far in the lead of any other class.

This could not have come at a more opportune time as Preachers all over are telling us that there is a gradual weaning away from the Church. If this will only make people think just for a little it will have done worlds of good.

I have sometimes wondered if the Preachers themselves have not something to do with this. You hear or read a sermon nowadays and the biggest part of it is taken up by knocking or trying to prove the falseness of some other denomination. They say that the Catholics are Damned, that the Jews' religion is all wrong, or that the Christian Scientists are a fake, or that the Protestants are all out of step.

Now just suppose, for a change, they preached to you about the Lord and not about the other fellow's Church, for every man's religion is good. There is none of it bad. We are all trying to arrive at the same place according to our own conscience and teachings. It don't matter which Road you take.

Suppose you heard a Preacher say, "I don't care if you join my Church or the other fellow's across the street. I don't claim mine to be better or worse than any other. But get with somebody and try and do better." Hunt out and talk about the good that is in the other fellow's Church, not the bad, and you will do away with all this religious hatred you hear so much of nowadays. Then you will not only have one Fred Stone but Millions of them.

Besides, it's not that we need more people just to join Churches. It's that we need more Fred Stones, either in or out of a Church. For this Man's life is an object lesson to every Young Man or Boy starting out on a career in any line of business. Sincerity put him where he is. He never faked. No man his age in America has worked harder and been more conscientious.

Another coincidence that happened applies directly to this case. I was called on to testify in Court if I thought a certain Team of Popular performers were UNIQUE AND EXTRAORDINARY. The whole case was based on those two words. Now those two words mean a terrible lot. They mean you must do something that no one else can do. So, regardless of the popularity of the two performers and with all due regard for all that others can do, I said they were not.

And I claim that the only one I know of in our entire profession who I could rightly claim was unique and Extraordinary is this man that went into a store and asked for a Bible. Went out and studied it according to his best knowledge. (Which, by the way, is not so much as Book learning goes. As Fred and I have figured up once. He got as far as the fourth reader while I only reached the third. So that is why I think we always hit it off together so well, neither was liable to use a word which the other couldn't understand.)

Fred Stone can do more things and do them well than any man in or out of the Show Business or the Movies.

Why can he?

He is 49 years old and has spent 45 years practicing. Now, we have not another man in America that has done that. He started at 4 or 5 years of age and has worked on new stunts every day of his life and still does. He always wanted to have something new for the people every year. We have performers that have specialized on one thing that are great, but not a one that can do the variety of things that he can. And the wonderful part is it is clean wholesome entertainment that you are glad to have your children see. So the clean does pay after all in any line of business.

He was the originator of the present style of eccentric Dancing on the Stage. In his dances he dances not only with his feet but also his Body and face show you what he is trying to convey. The greatest compliment I ever heard paid a dancer was said about him by another great dancer, "Why Fred Stone can dance in a Barrel where you can't see his feet and still be a greater dancer to look at than the rest of them out of one."

A corking good all-around Acrobat. He practiced for years just to get a perfect One Hand Stand and never used it—just wanted to learn it. He is one of the best Actor Ball Players. Boxed for years with Corbett, who has always said that Fred could have been Champion at his weight.

Here's a little tip for you, too. He can lick more men single handed, if they start something

IF A RIDER HIT ON HIS HEAD, IT WAS ME.

with him, than can any Hero in the Movies where they are trained to fall.

He took up Fancy Rope throwing after he was 37 years old and today there are not a half dozen Boys in this Country that can do more tricks than he can. He learned in 12 years what it's taken me 40 to learn. Hired Rinks to stay open after their seasons closed and paid Instructors for three years to perfect him in fancy Ice Skating. He learned Bareback Riding for a Circus Act, and every kind of Wild West trick riding. Bucking Horses he learned to ride after he was 43, just when at that age most Riders are quitting. He Bull Dogged a Steer at Cheyenne and had never done it before in his life. Now that takes nerve. I wouldn't jump off a horse on a steer even if he promised to lay down. He is a good Polo Player; we had a team composed of the late Vernon Castle, who, by the way was a good Horseman and a nervy fellow, Leo Corrello, Fred and Myself. Well, in our Clown games we all took it as a joke, but Fred took it serious. He wanted to know the thing from every angle.

Now to me I didn't care whether I hit the Ball or not. I knew it would be laying there when I come back. But not so with Fred. Well, there was a lot of falls and spills. The audience who watched us play every Sunday got to learn that in a spill if the falling Rider hit on his feet it was Fred Stone. If he hit on his head it was me. We would both be equally safe.

He is one of the best shots in the Country, has practiced for years with Annie Oakley, the Greatest shot this Country ever saw. He hunted big Game with his Brother-in-Law, Rex Beach, in Alaska. Went to Greenland to Lassoo, not shoot, Polar Bears, hunted Mountain Lions in Arizona, and Bears wherever he could hear of one.

Now that he has taken up religion and the Bible, he wont have to ask a Preacher to advise him long. Preachers will be coming to him, for he don't half do anything. So when he comes back, and Sunday comes, and I go down to Rope and Ride and play, if he wants to knock off and go to Church I don't think I will mind, and if they will let ME in, I may go too.

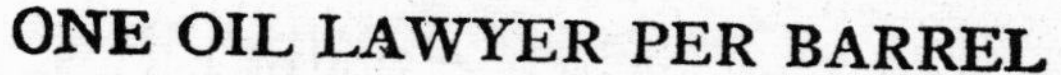

ONE OIL LAWYER PER BARREL

IT'S A BIGGER THING FOR WASHINGTON THAN THE SHRINER'S CONVENTION.

ONE OIL LAWYER PER BARREL

THE *Illiterate Digest* has devoted its life work to ferreting out the Persons and things in our National affairs which are not just exactly up to snuff. Now I see where the Senate Investigating Committee has called a recess for 10 days. Scandals were unfolding themselves so fast that the Committee couldn't get one Bribe straight in their minds before another one would bob up. So they retired to kinder see where they were at.

Now, while that committee may be resting, the *Illiterate Digest* never rests; we are on the heels of the evildoer 24 hours of every bribing day. I hope by the time this reaches an eager waiting Public that they will have found two Lawyers to conduct this Oil investigation. Just think, America has one hundred and ten million population, 90 percent of which are Lawyers, yet we can't find two of them who have not worked at some time or another for an Oil company. There has been at least one lawyer engaged for every barrel of Oil that ever come out of the ground.

You might wonder if they pay so much to Lawyers

how do they ever make anything out of the Oil? Foolish question. They don't make anything out of the Oil. They only make money out of the stock they sell. You buy a share of oil stock and for every dollar you pay, 60 percent goes for Lawyers' fees, 30 percent to over Capitalization, and 10 percent goes to the boring of a Dry Hole.

If a Company just put down Wells for Oil, and then sold the oil legitimately, they would have no use at all for Lawyers. But Oil Men engage their Lawyers nowadays even before they have leased the land or know where they are going to prospect. For the lawyer has to make the lease. It's not like any other business where the owner and the man who is going to lease can meet and do business. Oh no, Lawyers must do that. Then, if they happen to be leasing from the Government, why they not only have to be Lawyers but have to be Political Lawyers.

Now, I bet a lot of you thought after the Company had got the land leased, that the next thing to do was to hire a Driller to put the Well down. But you are wrong again. You go out and get another Lawyer. You have to have another Lawyer to draw up the contract with the driller.

THEY NOT ONLY HAVE TO BE LAWYERS, BUT POLITICAL LAWYERS.

Then I bet that you think the next step is to wait until you see whether you have Oil or not. Say, don't make me laugh out loud again. You don't wait for anything of the kind: you engage another Lawyer to draw up some pretty Oil Stock Paper with nice flowered edges. Looks like a marriage license—only worse. Then you start selling the stock, claiming that the BoHunk Oil Company are putting down a Well on Smith 29, North East 40 of South West 80. Then if they do strike something, they shut it up and claim it was a Duster.

Then they get another Local Lawyer who knows everybody around that neck of the Woods, to go out and buy up or lease all the adjoining land. Then, when they get it all leased, they go back and pick the stopper out of this. Well, double the Capitalization of Stock under the direction of still another Lawyer, and then they are in a position to hire more Lawyers to investigate getting a Lease from Persia, or Jugo-Slavia. This just kinder gives you a rough idea of what all these Lawyers do and why we can't get any to help prosecute this Oil Scream.

The *Illiterate Digest* will have to take Editorial attention of the resignation of Sectry Denby. Mr.

Denby was requested by the Senate to resign. Now that in itself is a mighty good Omen that he is an unusually able man. Of course, where I think he got in bad was in saying, if he had the same thing to do over again he would do it. It is always bad for any one on trial to say he would do the same thing over again. American People like to have you repent; then they are generous.

But you see lots of times a man gets in wrong just by an ill timed remark. Look at Mr. Doheny's reported remark that he would "make 100 million out of the Elk Hills lease." That will go down in History as the highest priced Gag ever pulled. That's why Mr. Coolidge never gets in bad. If a man will just stay hushed he is hard to find out.

Personally and Editorially, I don't think Mr. Denby is guilty at all of any wrong-doing that he knew of. But somebody has got to go in this thing, and before it's all over you are mighty apt to find a few innocent along with all the guilty strewn along by the Pipe Line.

By the way, sometime this Country, just by accident, is going to get some man Sectry of the Navy who has at least received a Picture Post Card of Annapolis, sometime during his career. Josephus

Daniels had never been in anything bigger than a Row Boat up to the time he was made Sectry of the Navy. The first Battleship he got on he kept looking for the Paddle Wheels on the side that made it go. He found the Officers in those days had Cocktail and Cordial Glasses with their Table wear. He made them throw them all overboard. He thought they would sink the Ship. What he lacked in seamanship, he made up in morality.

Then came Mr. Denby who had received his Maritime Education by looking at the Detroit River (which is so thick with Booze Boats that you can't see the Water) naturally his Aquatic viewpoint is rather warped.

I guess Young Theodore Roosevelt comes nearer being an Old Salt than anyone connected with our Ex Oil Owners (The Navy). He did live in Oyster Bay overlooking Long Island Sound, and had to look at the Joy Line cruising, 1$ daily, to Providence. Then he had to Subway under the East River to get to New York. So I guess he is the only Sectry we have that knows just by looking at one, which end of a Battleship is the front.

Judging by the previous experience of some of our sectrys, of various things in our Cabinets, it has always been a source of great anxiety to me just why a Vetenerian has never been appointed either Sectry of War or PostMaster General.

Now by the time this reaches our Scandal loving Public I don't know who will be left in Washington. The chances are, when I visit the old stamping ground again, I will have to make entirely new acquaintances. But I will always have the feeling, "Well the old Boys were not so bad. They were just unfortunate in getting caught."

It certainly looks like a tough year. Politicians are so busy trying to hold down their own Jobs that they won't have any time to look out for any-one else. They will be voting a Bonus to men who lost their livelihood in the great morality Panic of 1924.

Children in future years will ask their Parents, "Father how much did you get in the great Year 1924?"

It's been a fine thing for Washington. The Hotels are crowded. Every time a Guest registers the Clerk asks him, "I suppose you will be here until you testify." It's a bigger thing for Washington than the Shriners' Convention, because it has all of them, besides a lot more.

If they would all tell the truth the first time they testify they wouldn't have to testify again like they are doing now, and they would get the thing over a lot quicker. They ought to pass a rule in this Country that in any investigations, if a Man couldn't tell the truth the first time he shouldn't be allowed to try again.

Now we have another Scandal in the Veterans' Bureau. But we are just in such shape that we can't take care of but one Scandal at a time. If any other small affairs come up during the coming season that look like they might develop into a Scandal I will try to let you know.

ANOTHER HOT CONFESSION IN THE OIL SCANDAL

THEY ARE FROM TULSA. I WILL BE RIGHT OUT.

ANOTHER HOT CONFESSION IN THE OIL SCANDAL

I WISH this Oil Scandal would hurry up and be settled as it is very hard for one writing on affairs of our Country to tell, in writing of our Officials, whether to speak of them as Secretary So and So, or Ex-Secretary So and So. Up to now I claim a very unique distinction. I am the only Person I know of that has not been mentioned as receiving something in the nature of a Fee from some Big Corporation. But I am going to get in early and tell just what I received so when my name comes up later on people will say: "Well there is a Man who has accepted Fees but he was honest about them and come to the front and told it." As I can't get to Washington to testify I want to tell through the Digest, for which I am Scandal Correspondent, just what happened to me. If I was in Washington I probably couldn't get to testify as there is so many ahead of me that it will take years for just the People who work for the Government to tell who gave them something.

I know a Man that went to Washington to testify

as to money he had received and there was 29 Cabinet and Ex Cabinet Members in line ahead of him so he had to just write it and send it in. Now this whole thing was a strictly Republican affair until Mr. Doheny (who never lets Politics interfere with his Business) appeared before the Commission, and when it looked like he was the only Oil be-spattered sheep in the Democratic Fold, he just kicked over an Oil Can and hiding behind it were a flock of Democrats that reached almost as far back as Jefferson's Administration.

Personally I am glad that he did unearth members of both Parties for if this thing had gone through showing no one but Republicans, it would have cast a reflection on the shrewdness of the Democratic Party. In other words they would have looked rather dumb to be standing around with all these Oily Shekels falling all around them and not opening their Pockets to catch a few. For the American people are a very generous people and will forgive almost any weakness, with the possible exception of stupidity.

But to get back to my confession for I want to be set right before the people by the time we meet in Madison Square Garden in June to select the worst man. Mine starts out like a Fairy Story.

Once upon a time, I had just gone to work for Florenz Ziegfeld, Jr., and was playing in what was called Ziegfeld's Midnight Frolic, on the Roof of the Amsterdam Theatre, New York. Prohibition and my Jokes were equally responsbile in closing the place up. Now my home is (as I think I mentioned before) Claremore, Oklahoma, (The home of the best Curative Waters in the World) and, by the way, one of the best towns in the World to live in if any of you are thinking about making a change.

Well, after I had finished my little 15 minutes of annoyance in the Frolic one night, one of the Waiters (for instead of having Ushers to hand you a Programme, they had Waiters to hand you a drink, and I tell you, you can't beat some of the old customs). Well this well tipped Waiter come to my dressing room, which I used to hang my ropes in, and said, "There is a Party of folks out front at one of the Tables from Oklahoma, and they want you to come out and see them." I asked what place in Oklahoma did they come from, and he said, "I don't know but they certainly got the Dough; they have ordered everything in the place but the Kitchen Stove." I said, "They are from Tulsa. I will be right out."

Well I hid what few dollars I had down in my Sock, and went out to see them. It was Mr. Harry Sinclair. I had never heard of him before, for he hadn't bought Zev or the Teapot Dome up to then. But we soon felt like we knew each other, on account of him being from Tulsa (a Residential Suburb of Claremore where we park our millionaires to keep them from getting under our feet). He knew my Father who had been a member of the Constitutional Convention, which drafted the Charter of Oklahoma.

Well, this Mr. Sinclair was an awful nice fellow. We hit it off pretty good. We kinder consoled each other, on account of being so far from home, and trying to eke out an existence from these shrewd New Yorkers. He took a fatherly interest in me, and asked, "Now, Will, you are working here but what are you doing with your money?" So I told him just what I was doing with it, that the last three months' wages had gone to paying a Doctor and a Nurse, for assisting us in accumulating another Baby, and that the three months previous to that my wages had gone to making the first payment on a second hand Overland car, and that the year still previous to that I had bought a Baby Buggy and a Victrola.

Well, he seemed mighty pleased that I was putting my money into such staple commodities. So I asked him what he was doing with his. He said, "I struck Oil, but Oil is no good unless its Capitalized."

Well, that was news to me. I thought you could just sell the Oil itself. But I learned that you can get twice as much for the Capital as you can for the Oil.

So then he asked me the names of my Private Herd. I told him I had gone to a great deal of trouble and thought in naming them and after months of research among pretty and odd names of Novels and Poems, I had decided to name the Children, Bill, Mary and Jim.

Well, he had never heard of anything more original. The names I thought struck him very odd, as he wrote all three of them down on the back of an Envelope. So I left the Table as I didn't want to be there when the Waiter presented his check. For I had seen several Casualties from this same cause.

I never thought much more about it. I went home and told my Wife about meeting him, and what do you think happened! In a couple of days here comes three official letters addressed to Bill, Mary and Jim, and they had enclosed a Share each of Sinclair Oil Stock *free*. Well we thought that was a mighty fine thing for him to do to be so thoughtful of our little Tribe. I accepted it in as good faith as McAdoo did his Fee.

I don't know if the Senate investigating Committee will get around to them soon or not. Of course they will have to get through before Election for the whole thing will be a total loss after election. All I have to say is that the Children were Private Citizens and did not promise to use any influence in any way. Of course, I, as the Father and Guardian of the Children, will be apt to come in for considerable criticism, and I may go so far as to lose any chance I may have as being named as a Presidential possibility.

Now I hate this for the Children's sake that all this must come out for it is liable to put a stigma on their names that they will be two Campaigns living down. One thing, of course, will be in their favor when it all does come out and that is that it was sent openly through the mails. It was not delivered in a Suit Case.

They have had these shares for years and have also received at various times a Dollar or so Interest on said Stock. When this Expose came out Bill and Mary were for resigning and sending in their Stock, so they could show that they were not connected with the Corporation, but Jim, the youngest, who has a touch of Republicanism in him, why, he said, "No, let's stick until they throw us out. Let them prove we took these Stocks for some other reason than Charity!"

What makes it look bad is, that my Wife wrote a note and thanked him. But the children did not sign the Note. So when he is called upon to testify he will have her Note but it won't have the Children's Signature on it. Of course he can say it was tore off, or that his Wife has that part of it, or some other equally good reason. But I want the Public to be lenient with both him and the Children, for as past events have proven they haven't done a thing for him to warrant them getting those Stocks. So I honestly believe he meant no harm when he gave them.

As for Mr. Doheny giving me or mine anything,

we live right near him here in Beverly Hills. His son did promise me a key, so I wouldn't have to ride clear around his Estate when out horseback riding, but I never got it yet.

THE WHOLE TRUTH AND NOTHING BUT THE TRUTH

I OBJECT TO THE SENATOR FROM MASSACHUSETTS' SLURRING REMARKS.

Comedy Drama

Entitled

THE WHOLE TRUTH AND NOTHING BUT THE TRUTH

PLACE—Washington, D. C.

TIME—From 1924 to 1930.

SCENE—One of the 40 Investigating Rooms of the U. S. Senate.

CAST OF CHARACTERS—Everybody that ever worked for, or just Worked the United States.

HERO—Senator Walsh, assisted by Lenroot and accomplices.

VILLAINS—Entire list of Who's Who in America.

The Scene opens on a greasy Monday morning with JOHN F. MAJOR *being quizzed by* SENATOR WALSH.

SENATOR WALSH

Do you work for a Man that runs a Newspaper?

MR. MAJOR

I draw a salary from him.

SENATOR WALSH

What right have you to send Telegrams to a Man in Palm Beach if you are only working for him?

MR. MAJOR

I couldn't get him on the Telephone.

SENATOR WALSH

What did you tell him in your Telegrams?

MR. MAJOR

What was going on in Washington.

SENATOR WALSH

What did he tell you in his Telegrams to you?

MR. MAJOR

What was going on in Palm Beach.

SENATOR WALSH

What was going on at the time in Washington?

MR. MAJOR

Why the Senate Committee was investigating somebody.

SENATOR WALSH

Who were they investigating?

MR. MAJOR

They didn't know themselves.

SENATOR WALSH

What did he say was going on in Palm Beach?

MR. MAJOR

I am ashamed to tell you.

SENATOR WALSH

Who were these Telegrams from in Palm Beach?

MR. MAJOR

I can't remember.

SENATOR WALSH

Did you lease a Wire from Palm Beach to Washington?

MR. MAJOR

I can't remember.

SENATOR WALSH

Why did you lease the Wire?

MR. MAJOR

So we could say we had a Wire to Palm Beach. It was good advertising.

SENATOR WALSH

Who operated this wire?

MR. MAJOR

A Telegraph Operator.

SENATOR WALSH

What was his name?

MR. MAJOR

I think it was Jones, or Smith; maybe it was Brown.

SENATOR WALSH

Who operated the wire from Palm Beach?

MR. MAJOR

Johnny.

SENATOR WALSH

Johnny who?

MR. MAJOR

Johnny Johnnnny.

SENATOR WALSH

Did the operator on this end work at the White House also?

MR. MAJOR

Yes he was the Waiter there.

SENATOR WALSH

Did he work there during the Republican or Democratic Administration?

SENATOR LODGE

Mr. Committee, I object to that question. This is not a Partisan affair; I refuse to have the honor and the glory of the Great Republican Party dragged into a thing where up to now their fair name has never been.

SENATOR CARAWAY

Mr. Committee, I object to the Senator from Massachusetts' slurring remarks of the Democratic

Party; a Party which has housed such illustrious names as Jefferson, Cleveland, Akron, Youngstown, Bryan, McAdoo, and sometimes Jim Reed.

MR. MAJOR

Senator Walsh have you got a Cigarette on you?

SENATOR WALSH

No I just got some cubebs here.

MR. MAJOR

Never mind I will go across the Street and get some. See you next time I am called.

SENATOR WALSH

Gentlemen, I think the Committee should retire for a week to consider the Testimony of the Gentleman who has just testified.

SENATOR LENROOT

But Mr. Chairman, Mr. Doheny's Yacht is waiting to take him on a Cruise of the Mediterranean, and I don't think it's fair to keep him waiting.

SENATOR WHEELER

Mr. Chairman, I make a motion, that the Committee make a motion, that Attorney General Daugherty resign.

SENATOR LODGE

Mr. Chairman, I object. His motion is out of order. I had a motion before the Committee asking the Committee asking the Committee to make a motion, to ask him to stay. Now, by all the rules of Parliamentary motion making, mine anti-dates his. And I will stake a Reputation on it that goes back to the first class Passengers that landed from that Mother Ship of mine the Mayflower, who have so gloriously populated the fair state of Massachusetts.

SENATOR ROBINSON

Mr. Chairman, I object. The fair state of Arkansas houses one direct descendant of that Plymouth Rock Expedition. And I protest when the Gentleman from Massachusetts claims the entire Cargo of that ill-fated Voyage. Never as long as I represent the majority constituency of my Glorious state will I stand by and hear the ozone swept Ozarks spoken of disparagingly, especially by that Moron State of Massachusetts.

SENATOR WILLIS

Gentlemen, I don't think that Mr. Daugherty should be let out without a trial.

SENATOR WHEELER

Why, he has had three year's trial already. His trial is what's letting him out.

SENATOR WALSH

Who will we call next?

DOORTENDER

Why just get a Census return, and call anybody's name on it; they are waiting outside.

SENATOR LA FOLLETTE

Why don't you call somebody unexpectedly, and maybe in their confusion they will tell the truth accidentally.

SENATOR LENROOT

Who said anything about wanting the truth?

SENATOR HEFLIN

I want to ask the Committee why they called on Mr. Fall at his hotel in private.

SENATOR WALSH

We wanted to see where he got the hundred thousand. We may retire ourselves some day.

SENATOR HEFLIN

Why didn't you tell at the time that you went to see him?

SENATOR WALSH

Wait a minute, who is running this investigation? Am I supposed to ask the questions, or to answer them?

SENATOR LENROOT

Where is Sinclair?

MR. ZEVERLY

(whose running name is Zev.)

My Client, Mr. Sinclair has gone to the races and it will be impossible for him to appear until after the season is over.

SENATOR WALSH

Well how about McLane? Can we get him?

SENATOR CARAWAY

You can get him by Telegraph, I guess. Everybody else has.

SENATOR WALSH

Well, where is Detective William J. Burns? He was supposed to testify here today.

DOORTENDER

Mr. Chairman, I met him on the Street and he couldn't find the Capitol Building.

SENATOR MOSES

I make a motion that we examine the Income Tax and see what Mr. Doheny contributed to the Democratic Campaign Fund.

SENATOR JIM REED

I object. Senator Moses is a Republican and he is only throwing a smoke Screen to try and hide his Party behind it. This is not a Partisan question and I object to politics being dragged into it in any way. Let's handle this thing in a dignified way, and don't let Politics play any part. As it was the Republicans that did it, I am in favor of justice being served.

DOORTENDER

Mr. Forbes is here and wants to testify.

ENTIRE SENATE

"My Lord, Is he in this, too?"

P. S.—This play to be continued until somebody tells the truth.

WELL, WHO IS PRUNES?

"THERE'S A BELLBOY AT MY HOTEL AND HE JUST GOT IT FROM THE CHAUFFEUR OF A PROMINENT OIL-MAN."

WELL, WHO IS PRUNES?

2nd Episode of the great Dramatic Serial,

THE TRUTH, NOTHING BUT THE TRUTH, SO HELP ME GOD.

Same scene as the first Episode—the Third Degree Room of the Grand Jury of the United States Senate. MR. SENATOR WALSH *leading question asker of a body of men noted for their inquisitiveness.*

DOORTENDER OF THIS TORTURE CHAMBER

Who will we call first today?

SENATOR WALSH

Call the Editorial Writer of that newspaper.

DOORMAN

But, Mr. Walsh, we just called him yesterday.

SENATOR WALSH

I know we did but call him again. A whole lot is happening in this country between yesterday and today. Now Mr. Bennett who was it that you referred to as the Principal in those wires to Palm Beach?

MR. BENNETT

Why, Senator Curtis.

SENATOR HEFLIN

Curses on the Luck. I thought it was Coolidge.

SENATOR HARRISON

Wish it had of been Coolidge. It's no novelty to get a Senator in Wrong.

SENATOR WALSH

What did you confer with Curtis about?

MR. BENNETT

About the Editorial Policy of our Paper.

SENATOR WALSH

Well what does the Editorial Policy of any Paper amount to? You don't suppose anybody reads those things do you? Why one Ad is worth more to a paper than 40 Editorials. That will be all for you Mr. Bennett.

SENATOR CARAWAY

Just a minute before you go. Who was Peaches in those Telegrams?

MR. BENNETT

I don't remember.

SENATOR ROBINSON

Yes, and who was Prunes? I hope it referred to no Democrat.

SENATOR WALSH

Call Mr. Curtis.

SENATOR WALSH

Senator Curtis, will you tell the Grand Jury in your own way just what happened between you and this Editorial Writer of the Washington *Post*.

MR. CURTIS

Yes Sir.

SENATOR WALSH

What was it?

MR. CURTIS

Nothing.

SENATOR WALSH

You mean you didn't confer with this Gentleman?

MR. CURTIS

I did not.

SENATOR WALSH

But you know him?

MR. CURTIS

Never saw him in my life.

SENATOR WALSH

But you have heard of him?

MR. CURTIS

Never in my life.

SENATOR WALSH

But you know of the Washington *Post*?

MR. CURTIS

Yes sir, I have heard it.

SENATOR WALSH

Heard it? What do you mean you heard it?

MR. CURTIS

I have heard Sousa's Band play it many a time.

SENATOR WALSH

Play what?

MR. CURTIS

Washington's Post.

SENATOR WALSH

It's not a tune; it's a Newspaper. You talk like a Congressman. Where are you from?

MR. CURTIS

Kansas.

SENATOR WALSH

That will be all.

SENATOR CARAWAY

Just a minute, Mr. Curtis, Who is Peaches?

MR. CURTIS

I don't know unless it's Jim Reed.

SENATOR HEFLIN

Just a minute. I object to the Republican Senator's slur on the fair name of the Democratic Party. This Investigation is supposed to be Non Sectarian, and I object to having Politics dragged in, just to make a Republican Holiday.

SENATOR ROBINSON

And I want to know who Prunes was.

MR. CURTIS

You mean you want to know who Prunes IS.

SENATOR LENROOT

Mr. Walsh, and Gentlemen of the Vigilance Committee there is a Bell Boy over at my Hotel and he just got it from the chauffeur of a Prominent Oil Man, that Major Leonard Wood's Son had just heard that his Father was offered the Nomination for the Presidency 3 and a Half years ago, if he would appoint Mr. Jake Hamon Secretary of the Interior. Now that is a very serious charge, and one that I think this Committee should look into at once. Public affairs have come to a fine Climax when a Man in this Country offers to make another one President. I tell you it is undermining the confidence of the Great American People and when you do that you shake the very Bulwarks of the American Constitution. I think a Subpœna should be issued for Mr. Wood's Son at once and if this is so I am for a swift and speedy trial for the Culprits.

SENATOR WALSH

I am for calling Mr. Wood himself. There's one thing that this Committee has proven that it won't take, and that is Hear Say Evidence. So call Mr. Wood himself.

MR. MOSES

(The Senator one, Not the Apostle One)

But, Mr. Walsh, Mr. Wood is in the Philippines.

SENATOR WALSH

I thought he was home. Haven't they got their Independence yet?

MR. MOSES

No, Mr. Coolidge wouldn't give it to them.

SENATOR WALSH

What's the matter? Have they struck oil, too?

MR. MOSES

No, Mr. Coolidge told them that a Nation that would not support Wood's Administration certainly would not be able to support one of their own.

SENATOR HEFLIN

Well, how did America get Independence? They didn't support Wood.

SENATOR REED

Who said we had any independence?

SENATOR LODGE

(The Confucius of Nahant)

I object to having the President of these United States' name dragged into this thing. I think when a Man occupies the exalted position that he does that his name should not be degraded by having it mentioned in The Senate. Now I know that he is doing the best he can. I have known him ever since he got prominent enough for me to know. In the eight months that I have known him, I have found him to be patient, honest, and a Man who would not knowingly rob a single Filipino of his Liberty. This is simply a Political trick to drag his name into this Philippine muddle.

SENATOR HEFLIN

Yes but he sent the Filipinos the Wire didn't he! And it's wires that we are here to investigate ain't it?

SENATOR HARRISON

Does the exalted Senator from Massachusetts recall that during the late Democratic Administration, he himself during the talk on European Affairs mentioned not only once, but twice, the name of the then President, Mr. Wilson? Now he don't want us to mention his President.

SENATOR HEFLIN

Well it's funny to me that a Country can't get their Liberty, when they have advanced far enough to have the Champion Bantamweight Prize Fighter of the World. I know Countries that have their Liberty, when they can't even produce a good Golf Player and that's the lowest form of Civilization.

SENATOR CARAWAY

I would like to ask Mr. Lodge if he knows who Peaches is.

SENATOR LODGE

I do not. It's the only subject I ever admitted being ignorant on.

SENATOR ROBINSON

Well, I want to know who Prunes IS.

SENATOR LODGE

You mean who Prunes AM, don't you?

SENATOR ROBINSON

Darn it; that man is a bear on Grammar.

SENATOR WALSH

I think the committee should adjourn until we can get Mr. Wood himself.

DOORMAN

Excuse me, Mr. Walsh, but there is a Gentleman

out here who wants to testify in regard to the Doheny and Sinclair leases. What can I tell him?

SENATOR WALSH

Oh, yes, I had forgotten about those. Tell him as soon as we get this Wood for President affair settled, and Jack Dempsey's mysterious sickness, and Babe Ruth's collapse, that we will be able to get to that Oil Lease thing again.

SENATOR COPELAND

Mr. Walsh, I was in New York last night and I heard Mr. Vanderlip make a Speech to the Rotary Club of Coney Island, and he said, "I have it on absolutely reliable authority that George Washington never crossed the Delaware. That fellow you see in the Picture in the middle of the Boat was a fellow doubling for him, and if I am called I will be glad to give this information that I possess to the Senate Investigating Committee."

SENATOR WALSH

Mr. Secretary, call Mr. Vanderlip at once.

MR. LENROOT

Let's not call him until tomorrow, Mr. Walsh, as he will make another speech tonight perhaps on what he discovered about Lincoln. So we can quiz him on both men at once.

MR. CARAWAY

Well, before we adjourn, I want to know who Peaches is.

MR. ROBINSON

Well, I want to know who Prunes WERE.

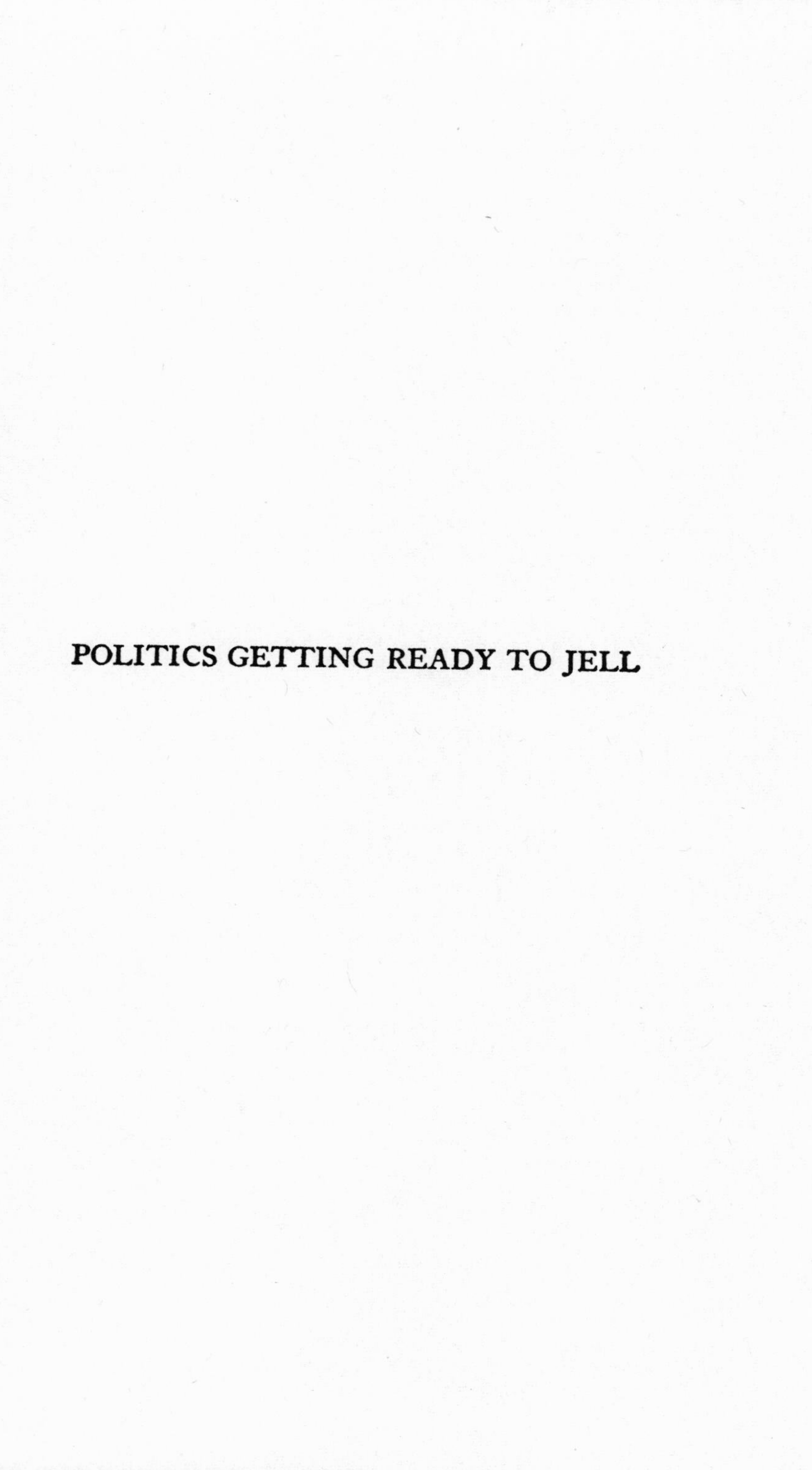

POLITICS GETTING READY TO JELL

POLITICS GETTING READY TO JELL

THE Illiterate Digest, after reviewing the news, finds that Politics is sure at the point when it is about to jell. My old friend Jim Reed from the smelly banks of the Kaw River has broke out again. If you have done anything against the welfare or conventions of the United States, and everybody has passed their various opinions on you, and you think you have been roasted to a dark bay, why, until Jim Reed breaks out on you, you haven't been called anything.

Well, it was kinder funny Jim was to make a Washington Day speech. Naturally everyone supposed it to be on George Washington, but it was the only speech ever made on Washington's Birthday that didn't have a word about Washington. He didn't even mention his name. I don't know that McAdoo, Denby, Daugherty, Doheny, and others will consider it much Flattery, but it will go down in History as being the only time they ever replaced Washington.

Reed wouldn't have been any good making a

speech on Washington, anyway. He would have been expected to compliment him and I doubt if he could think of anything George had ever done that really was worth while.

Vanderlip made a speech at the Rotary Club of Ossining, New York, that astonished the United States. Now that speech didn't astonish me near as much as the knowledge that Ossining *had* a Rotary Club. For the sake of the unfingerprinted ones, I will state that Ossining is the Town where Sing Sing is permanently located. Now if Ossining has a Rotary Club they certainly had to take in some Lay Members from this Musically named Institution.

But when you come to think of it, just think what a Distinguished Rotary Club they could have at that. Rotary is composed of one of the best of each line of work or business. Just think what a competitive thing it would be trying to find in Ossining the leading Burglar sojourning with them at the time, or the most representative Pickpocket to represent them in the Club. And Bankers! Mr. Vanderlip must have felt right at home up there. There are more Bankers in Ossining than any Town of its size in the United States.

A two year residence is necessary to be able to join the Rotary. Can you imagine them questioning members of Sing Sing, "Have you been a resident of this Town for two years?" and the answer would be, "Yes Sir, constantly."

So, as I say, it was not the things Mr. Vanderlip said that attracted the unusual attention. It was the distinguished audience that he delivered it to. Just to show you the difference: Appearing before the Rotary Club of Sing Sing he caused a commotion by his Speech. He took the same Act down to Washington and nobody would listen to him. It shows you have to have an intelligent audience. Up in Sing Sing they got what he was talking about but down in Washington it went right over their heads.

I know, for last winter while playing in New York I was asked to go over to a big Charity affair given by the 400 of 5th Avenue. I thought I had a pretty good line of Gags, as there was quite a lot happening every day of Public interest. So I go over and start in telling them what I had read in the Papers and nobody even cracked a smile, much less laughed. So I just kept on trying remarks on every subject that had been in the papers since Bryan last got a Hair cut. But it was about one of the worst Flops I ever encountered, and I have had some beauts in my time.

Well, of course, I felt terrible about it, so just by a coincidence on the very next night I had promised to go up to Ossining and do an act for (at that time it wasn't called the Rotary Club). I think then they called it Inmates. There was no show—just me alone went up to add to the hardships of Prison Life. Well I never knew I had as many friends in the World. I knew everybody up there. I was twice as much at home as I had been on 5th Avenue the night before. So now I know why Vanderlip picked out Ossining for his Annual February Oration.

I started in on those same Jokes on up-to-date things that had flopped so completely at the Millionaire's Charity affair. Why, say, they just started right in dying laughing at them. I was sorry Ziegfeld wasn't there, as I would have got a raise in salary if he had heard how my act went. I don't care what I talked about they knew all about it.

Ordinarily, I only do about 15 or 20 minutes but up there I did an Hour and a Quarter. I was so tickled I offered to take all the whole audience of 12 hundred down to the Follies and pay their way in to see our Show. Now you know I must feel pretty good with myself, when I offer to spend my Dough like that. A lot of people would be kinder sore at the 400 because they didn't laugh like these 12 hundred did, but I am not. I don't blame them. If I had their money I wouldn't read either. So I can understand very readily why Vanderlip's act didn't go so big in Washington as it did in Ossining.

Of course Van and I use just the opposite methods in our Stage performances. Every Gag I tell must be based on truth. No matter how much I may exaggerate it, it must have a certain amount of Truth. Vanderlip bases his Gags on Rumor.

Now Rumor travels Faster, but it don't stay put as long as Truth. I will, however, give him credit for one thing. While here lately everybody is telling what he has heard, and all about this and that rumor, why, he thought of by far the best ones I have heard up to now.

That's no small accomplishment I tell you, in this year of Rumors, to be able to say at the end of it: "Well, I told the best ones."

His were so good that before his audience got

through applauding at Sing Sing (or rather Ossining) why, they had him on the stand at Washington. That's the first time a Theatrical troup ever jumped from Ossining to Washington.

They even put him on ahead of Fall, Sinclair, and all the Headliners.

TWO LONG LOST FRIENDS FOUND AT LAST

THEY REHEARSED THEIR OLD ACT HERE YESTERDAY.

TWO LONG LOST FRIENDS FOUND AT LAST

WELL, sir, I have a real Message for my readers. It looked like it would be just the ordinary Article with no flavor or Backbone or Truth, and with no real underlying news or wisdom, that is, nothing that the people would be glad to know and read. As I say, that is the kind of Article I thought it would be. But as I picked up the morning Papers, why, I read who was in our midst out here in Sunny California. Well, sir, it struck me like a thunderbolt here was news which my public had been longing for for years and here I had found it out!

Well, I says to myself, this is too good to keep, for here people had been wondering all this time for just what I knew now. I kinder hated to leave the East on account of thinking I would be out of touch with some of our National Characters but I find that sooner or later they all arrive out here and start in fighting off Real Estate men the same as shooing away Mosquitoes on Long Island.

Well, who should blow in but two of our old long-lost friends, and I know that even 'Frisco (who is jealous of any one being here) will be glad to hear they are here well and hearty, and rehearsed their old Act here yesterday and people enjoyed them just as much as they did in the old days.

Both of these Boys were on the big time and were well known all around the Circuit, and any time they took the Platform standing by the side of a Pitcher of ice water and a glass, why, it just meant 6 columns starting on the front page and ending among the want ads. I bet you hadn't heard of them in years and will thank me for resurrecting this information for you.

I can't keep it any longer. I did want to keep it till the finish of this to tell you but I must tell you now who they are—William J. Bryan and Billy Sunday!

Neither did I, but *they are,* and looking fine.

You know, if you have lost any one, look out here, because sooner or later they will come here to visit relatives, for anybody that has relatives comes here so he can write back to other relatives.

They are both just resting here (so is everybody else). Mr. Bryan is waiting till he finds out where the next Democratic Convention will be held, and then be there ready to knock any aspiring Presidential Candidate on the head the minute it shows above the mob.

The only way they will ever fool W. J. is some presidential year decide not to run any one. Then it will be a good joke on him; he will have no one to object to.

Of course, now we don't hear much of Democratic Candidates, as both sides are busy watching to see what Cal. will do. When he first become President there seemed to be quite a Sentiment to nominate him again for Vice President.

Everybody was wondering how he would come out of the Coal strike situation, and figured his political life or death depended on how he decided, so he just fools everybody by appointing some other man to settle it. Now, no other President had ever been smart enough to think of a thing like that; they tried to do it themselves, so I think he will go a long ways. He figured, why should I get in wrong when I can get some man to do it for me, so he just looked around until he found some other fellow who had a political future.

He said, "Gifford, you go get in wrong with

which ever side you decide against." Now, the minute a Crisis comes up, all he has to do is to remember some Republican name and appoint him to settle it for him.

Now the only Crisis that Mr. Coolidge can possibly get into, himself, is running out of Republicans to appoint. In that case he would have to appoint a Democrat which would bring on a worse Crisis than the one he appointed him to settle

But I am not here to talk about Cal. and what he is doing. I am here to tell you of these two long lost Prodigals that I discovered in the wilds of this Village. They were preaching in a Pulpit. I guess that's why no one had seen them for so long. Both these Boys, in the good old days used to talk in a Tent. Now you can always attract a crowd in a Tent, for they figure that it might be a Circus. Come to think of it, their Acts were similar; either one of them could take a Dictionary and sink an enemy with words at 40 paces.

Bryan's speeches have been the only thing to look forward to at a Democratic Convention for years. He has sent more Presidential Candidates home without a Reception Committee meeting them than any Monologist living. He can take a batch of words and scramble them together and leaven them properly with a hunk of Oratory and knock the White House door knob right out of a Candidate's hand.

Bryan has made more Political speeches than Germany has Marks. He kissed, when they were Babies, every man and woman in the United States who is now up to the age of 45. He has juggled the destinies of America more than any two Presidents because he has the choosing or rejecting of them.

His career has varied from Non-intoxication to Evolution; his hobbies have jumped from Grape juice to Monkeys. He tries to prove that we did not descend from the Monkey, but he unfortunately picked a time when the actions of our people prove that we did. He, undoubtedly, is one of our greatest minds and in most of his Theories he has been just too far ahead of the mob.

He preached Prohibition at a time when it meant Political Suicide for himself. I bet the next Democratic Candidate for President, no matter how strong he may think he is, would rather have the support of W. J. Bryan than any doubtful State in the Union.

Now that brings to us his accomplice, Willie Sunday, who I discovered staggering from one of our Local Pulpits last Sunday. To some of you who can't or don't wish to remember, Billy passed out just as Andy Volstead made his entrance. Now Barnum invented the Tent, but Billy Sunday filled it. He can get more people into a tent than an Iowa Picnic at Long Beach, California.

He is the only man in Ecclesiastical or Biblical history that ever had to train physically, for a sermon. He brought more converts to Prohibition before the 18th Amendment come in, than the 18th Amendment has converted to Prohibition since it went in.

He is the first preacher to specialize on Liquor. While Bryan's oratorical wrath in the later years has been hurled at Darwin, Billy Sunday picks his opponent with a carelessness that is almost reckless.

I suppose that he has had more mortal worldly combats with the Devil himself than any man living. He has challenged the Devil publicly more times than Wills, the Negro, has Jack Dempsey. People have been going for years to hear Billy, just figuring that if they didn't go that night it might be the very night the Devil would hear what Billy was calling him and come up, and they might miss what would happen.

I don't know this Devil myself but if he heard Billy say these things and didn't come up and call him for it, I think less of him than Billy does. Of course, the Devil may be just good natured, and figure, well, he can't hurt *ME,* and if he can get anything out of it why let him go ahead.

Now, of course, you can get a fellow wrong. Billy used to lay all the drinking on to this Devil, and claimed that if we had Prohibition we could lick this Devil. Now we got Prohibition, I don't think he can legitimately lay the present drinking onto the Devil.

Course, from this I don't want you to think I am taking sides in this thing. I don't know either one personally. But, as I say, there is a chance that they both may have each other wrong. As I say, Billy must have something on the Devil or he wouldn't dare to call him what he does, especially if the Devil can hear him, and I tell you the Devil must be pretty low if he don't answer him, that is, if he hears him.

I have always figured that the reason that the Devil didn't arise and respond was Billy's slang was too much for him. But Billy sure did do a lot of good in the old days, and no matter if you didn't like his style of sermon, you sure didn't get a chance to do any sleeping.

So I hope we can keep them both out here with us, and help to get some of our population's mind on the Church on Sunday instead of being continually looking for lots.

THEY NOMINATED EVERYBODY BUT THE FOUR HORSEMEN

"YOU WASN'T HERE AND YOU KNOW THEM AS WELL AS I DO."

THEY NOMINATED EVERYBODY BUT THE FOUR HORSEMEN

AS I pen you these few lines, the Democratic National Convention is still going on; going on to where, nobody knows. But it has to end some time for even a Delegate can only stand just so much Oratory.

All the first week was taken up with seconding the nomination of McAdoo and Al Smith.

It looked like they were going to run out of people to do it, and they would have to second each other.

I wish you could have been there and heard what great men we have in this Country. We started out with 16 men for President. Here is what each one of them was.—"The only Man who can carry the Democratic Party to a Glorious Victory in November. Whose every act has been an inspiration to his fellow men. Not only loved in his Home State but in every State." Well, there was six continuous days of that.

Then the Ku Klux Klan argument come along, and really it was welcome even in New York. Just to get people's mind off that continuous, "The Man I am about to name to you."

One day and up to two thirty in the Night they fought and argued the Klan. It was the most exciting and Dramatic night I ever saw in my life.

After 11 hundred Delegates voted and recounted and voted the thing stood only about one vote apart, in fact a fraction of a vote, due to North Carolina, instead of having an election and naming 24 Delegates, just letting the whole State come as Delegates and giving each one the usual Volstead Ratio, Half of one percent of a Vote.

Alaska voted one Klu Klux away up there. Can you imagine a man in all that Snow and Cold with nothing on but a thin white Sheet and Pillow Slip?

My old Friend W. J. Bryan made one of his characteristic speeches. He said that if they split the Democratic Party with this Klan issue that another great Party would arise to take its place. Some guy up in the Gallery started Booing him. He just stopped and waited a minute until the heckler quit, then he said: "But no great leader of any Party has ever come from the Gallery." After that they laid off him.

Ex-Secretary of War Baker made a Speech on

the League of Nations and spoke of the 4 Horsemen of the Apocalypse, meaning I suppose, Borah, La Follette, Johnson and Brookhart.

I arrived late one morning, well only about 15 minutes late, and they had nominated five men for president already. I asked a Man in the Press stand who they were and he said, "You wasn't here and you know them as well as I do."

I had a friend who wanted to be nominated but all the nominating speakers were so given out that he had to let it go until next Election, that is in case they ever have another one.

If the one who is nominated can only swing the votes of the ones who were defeated he will give Mr. Coolidge a tight race.

Talk about Presidential Timber. Why, man, they had whole Lumber yards of it here.

There was so many being Nominated that some of the Men making the nominating Speeches had never even met the man they were nominating.

I know they had not from the way they talked about them.

Every time the speaker nominated somebody, why the Band would strike up what they thought was an appropriate tune. The bird nominated Gov.

Brown of New Hampshire kept talking and referring to "The Old Granite State. That Glorious old Granite State." When he finished the Band played "Rock of Ages". There was granite for you.

They nominated from a list of all Democrats. They drew them out the night before the convention.

Some Man named Stuart from Illinois got up to nominate somebody, and we knew we would hear something about Lincoln being born in Illinois, and sure enough we did. He kept quoting Lincoln's famous remark about, "God must have loved the common people because he made so many of them." Well this Bird kept talking about his man being for the common people, and he flopped terribly. You are not going to get people's votes nowadays by calling them common. Lincoln might have said it but I bet you it was not until after he was elected.

The fellow that nominated Charley Bryan from Nebraska was the only truthful one. He said, "I am going to nominate a Politician." You know nobody at these things dare mention Politician. Matchless leader or successor to Jefferson are about as low as they ever mention. This fellow told how

Bryan had lowered the price of Gasoline in Nebraska. And a crowd of people was seen to leave the hall. I think it was John D. Rockefeller and his Bible Class.

In the Charley Bryan demonstration staged by Nebraska, Florida joined in out of brotherly love.

When Bryan was presented the Band played "Way down Yonder in the Corn Field."

When Jimmy Cox was Nominated the band played, "Should Old Acquaintance Be Forgot." Jimmy Cox is a mighty fine man, But I don't know of any quicker way in the World to be forgotten in this Country than to be defeated for President. A Man can leave the Country and people will always remember that he went some place. But if he is defeated for President they can't remember that he ever did anything.

Smith's Demonstration lasted one hour and a Half. McAdoo's almost as long. But most of them just managed to last through a verse and one chorus by the Band.

Matthews of New Jersey nominated Gov. Silzer also of New Jersey. He made a plea for him on the ground that he came from the same state that President Wilson did. That don't mean anything.

Look I come from the same state that Harry Sinclair did. Yet I couldn't find an Oil Well without a search warrant.

His principal plea for Silzer was on the Highways of New Jersey. So if people west of the Mississippi and down south want a President who will keep the Roads of New Jersey up in good shape you can't do better than have him.

A guy from Utah talked so long and loud that all of us couldn't see how it could be anybody in the world he was nominating but Brigham Young that Matchless Father. But at the finish he crossed by saying he was seconding McAdoo's nomination.

You could never tell until one got through who he was going to name. They would pull the name last. That would be the only surprise they had.

Quinn of Minnesota throwed the biggest scare into the Convention. He praised his man so high that everybody in the hall knew it couldn't be anybody but La Follette but he fooled us all by seconding Smith. In his talk he never spoke of anything east of St. Paul and in Smith's travels he has never been west of Syracuse. So you see for yourself how hard it was to follow who they were going to name.

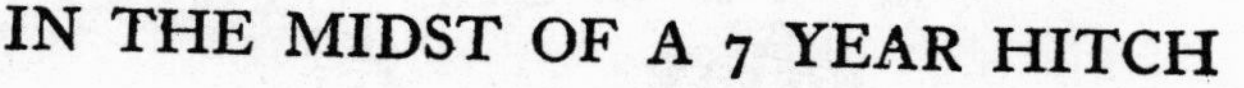

IN THE MIDST OF A 7 YEAR HITCH

WELL, I GUESS YOU HEARD ABOUT MY PRESIDENTIAL BOOM.

IN THE MIDST OF A 7 YEAR HITCH

WELL, I guess you heard about my Presidential Boom. You know every calamity in the World befell the Democrats while they were here in session the last couple of years. First they started in nominating. The entire first week was taken up with that. They nominated so many Democrats that if it had kept up another day they would have had to go over into the Republican Column. They talked their Delegates and audience to death the first week. No wonder they couldn't agree there was no two Delegates that could remember the same Candidate.

Well, it ran along week after week and the longer it ran the more confused the Delegates got. They began to get this Convention mixed up with the San Francisco one, because it had been so long since they left home, why, both Conventions seemed about the same distance off. One Delegation got to voting for Cox thinking it was 'Frisco. The Chairman had no more than got that straightened out and explained to them that this was an entirely different year when what does my Native State of Oklahoma do! They woke up the Chairman of their Delegation right quick one day to answer Roll Call and he blurts out, "Oklahoma votes 20 for Robert L. Owen." Well, the chairman had to explain to them that this was not 1920, and that Mr. Owen was not a Candidate, he was only a Delegate. The Missouri Delegation, when they could not get any two to agree, voted for two days for Champ Clark, until Telegrams commenced to pour in telling them of his demise.

Nebraska voted for Bryan, and got sore when the rest of the Convention thought it was W. J. They said it was a Son or a Brother or something of his. Mississippi and Louisiana started voting for my old friend Pat Harrison and Pat's Bottle run out, and they found an old Hoffman House Hotel Register, and from that on they just voted for the names on it.

Alabama was the only State that you could absolutely depend on. It seems that years ago Alabama sent a Delegation to some Convention instructed for a Candidate and that when they got there they sold out and voted for another. So they have passed a Law that any time they send a troup away again that they were going to vote for the man they told them to until the Candidate's body had been duly pronounced dead by the Home Coroner. Well, that knocked any chance of profit out of this trip as far as Alabama was concerned.

La Follette, out in Cleveland, wrote a Platform, held a Convention, nominated himself, and went home. All this happened during the time they were polling the Illinois Delegation here at this Convention.

Women Delegates started in with Bobbed Hair and wound up by being able to sit on it. One Woman sent back home for her washing machine. The Arkansas Delegation started in whittling up the Board floor and whittled their way from the Back of the Hall up to the Speaker's Platform. There was so many shavings under their Chairs that if a fire had ever broken out in the building, between these shavings and the long Whiskers, why, there would never in the World have been a way to stop it. There was one old long bearded Man from Utah, that when the voting on the Klan got close shook 4 Delegates with half a vote each out from under his Whiskers and decided the issue right there.

All the members of the National Committees had Gold Badges to start in with. The thing had only gone along a few weeks when they commenced to turn green and finally you couldn't tell whether it was a Badge or a Shamrock.

It's too bad because all the Delegates here will lose their votes when they go home this Fall. The law plainly states that you must have been a resident of the State for the last 6 months. If they were not thoughtful to register when they come to New York, they will lose their votes entirely.

Lots of the Delegates also had Wives who were Delegates, and this has been the longest time they ever spent together in their lives. I bet you will never see another Man go on a Delegation to a Democratic Convention when his Wife is on one. South Carolina has no Divorces, so of course this Convention gave all their members a chance to get out of the State, claim a residence of 6 months, and be divorced before they get home.

Now, mind you, as I pen these lines this thing is still going on. It's Monday morning of the third week. I don't know now who they will nominate. In fact people have lost interest. If they ever do nominate somebody some of the Papers may carry it

THE DEATHS FROM OLD AGE AMONG THE DELEGATES IS ABOUT OFFSET BY THE BIRTHRATE.

and you may know it by the time you read this, but I doubt if he will even be nominated by then. If he is, it will be too late to get his name on the Ballot by November, as the racing Forms have already gone to press for the November Classic. I am certainly glad that La Follette entered. That will give Coolidge somebody to run against, anyway.

If they don't hurry up they will be the only Party in the World that ever nominated a Candidate and got him defeated on the same day.

In number of Population the Convention is holding its own. The deaths from old age among the Delegates is about offset by the Birthrate. Personally I think that the Candidates who will finally be nominated will be born in this Convention.

I have been writing a daily account for the Papers for this seven years' Hitch. I took it for so much for the job. If I had signed by the word I would be able now to walk by and hiss Rockefeller.

In 1860, the Almanac says, a Democratic Convention was moved from Charleston to Baltimore. There is nobody here in this Convention to verify it, so I doubt if it ever happened. But, anyway, they talked for two Days about moving this one, on account of it being held here in New York where one of the Candidates lives. Well, they got to figuring and there was no Town they could take it to that didn't have a Candidate who lived there.

Of course their thoughts naturally turned to Claremore, Oklahoma, the best Town between Foyil and Catoosa in Oklahoma. Then when Arizona showed such splendid judgment in putting me in nomination, why of course we couldn't go there on account of the Galleries there being biased in favor of my nomination. Then they figured they might just as well stay here. Everybody had got used to the place, and if they moved them they would just have to get used to sleeping in strange chairs again, and maybe by a different seating arrangement they might be sleeping next to some one they didn't even know. It meant really a lot of trouble, anyway, opening up new credit accounts and getting used to a different Climate.

I want the Democrats to just pass this election by without getting beat and then center all their forces on 1928. Cal. will be ineligible then, unless they may pass a Constitutional amendment to elect a President for life—and he is so lucky they are just liable to do it. But if he is out, the Republicans will have to get a new man too. Then it will be an even break.

But go ahead with this Convention and pick him now. In fact I would pick out three or four to run in rotation in 1928, '32, '36, and so on, because you will never get Democratic Delegates to give up the best part of their lives by attending another one of these things. If they are wise today down there they will pick Jackie Coogan, for President and Baby Peggy for Vice President.

"WILL ROGERS JR." REPORTS THE CONVENTION FOR HIS FATHER, WORN OUT BY LONG SERVICE

(Mr. Rogers' articles on the Convention attracted more attention than perhaps any other humorous political articles. This one, in particular, brought him comments from all over the country.—THE PUBLISHERS.)

"WILL ROGERS JR." REPORTS THE CONVENTION FOR HIS FATHER, WORN OUT BY LONG SERVICE

WILL ROGERS JR. attended the convention to take up the duties of reporter to replace his venerable old father.

By WILL ROGERS JR.

Papa called us all in last night and made his last will and testament, he called it. He said he had carried his work on just as long as he could and he realized that he was unable, on account of his old age, to go further with it. He put in the will that I being the oldest was to take up his life's work, that of reporting the Democratic National Convention.

He herded us all and told us of how he had given all the best years of his life to this and out of respect to his name and memory that we children should carry on. And that our children were to do likewise and that we should raise them to always know that their mission through life would be to keep reporting the progress of the Democratic National Convention at New York. And it was in the will that if we didn't we would forfeit any claim to any royalties that might still be coming due from books that he had written on the early life of the convention.

Mama wants to send him to the Old Men and Old Women's Home for Survivors of this Convention, but he won't go. Poor Mama is worried about him. He won't talk rational. He just keeps saying, "Alabama" and "for what purpose does the gentleman arise," and "if we can't elect our candidate we will see that you don't get yours," and "unfit" and "release." We don't know what it all means.

Now, Mr. Editor, I am only a little boy and I am not much of a reporter, but Papa told us we didn't have to be very good; that all we must practice was endurance. But you will, Mr. Editor, please take my story, won't you for Mama's sake, for she knew how poor Papa hated to give up and how proud he will be if I can only keep his life's work going?

Mama got our Dad's old press badge and patched it up so it would stick together and I went down today. The hall was full of all those feeble people and it looked kinder like a church; everybody was sleeping. All but one man, who was standing and reading aloud out of a geography the names of States that are situated in the Western Hemisphere and that don't belong to Canada.

Papa had given me an old worn and torn paper with a list on it that he had used to mark off the numbers on when this convention started. He told me to always keep it for comparisons. Also that a museum had tried to buy it from him. I go to school and our teacher had told us what a wonderful country this is we live in, and how it had stuck so well together and, sure enough, when this man kept reading these names and figures, why, on Dad's old paper were a lot of the same ones.

I kept waiting for him to call out the name "Wisconsin" that Dad had, but this fellow didn't have it on his, and according to Dad's old paper we at that time had California and anybody knows that Japan has owned California for years. On Dad's old paper they still had the Philippine Islands, which is now Japan's Naval Base. But as for the candidates, the names were just the same. None of them had dropped out. Their sons were carrying on their father's life work too, trying to hold what votes they had. Saulsbury Jr. had six, Underwood Jr. had a few more than what was on Dad's paper, as the State of Alabama had more population and had naturally increased its number of delegates.

An old man sat by me and I got to talking to him and he seemed to want to be friendly and talk of his early life. He said his name was Coogan. "Jackie Coogan," I think he said, and that he used to be in some old fashioned things called moving pictures, and that he could remember as a child when this started that men used to be wakened up and have to call out the numbers when their States were called. But now they have little phonographs and every time a State is called, why the phonograph says "Two and nine-eighths for Smith Jr. and one and sixty-five fifths for McAdoo Jr." and so on.

A man has a hammer and he couldn't keep them awake with it any longer so they adjourned, and the attendants wheeled them all out. It was only about three o'clock in the afternoon and they were to be back again at nine. I went home to tell Pop what had happened and to write my story. He said, "It's looking better, son; they are adjourning earlier and starting later. Maybe the miracle will happen," and his old eyes began to gleam as he seemed to vision the end of his glorious dream.

Then I told him very enthusiastically, "Oh, yes, Pop, it looks great because a man with a family name of Brennan got up, and one named Cramer, and said they would adjourn and hold a conference of leaders and would have something to report by tonight."

Well, I wish you could have seen my poor old Dad. He went into spasms. He pulled his hair. He raved. None of us could do anything with him. He had been all right before I had mentioned this leader and conference business. He then said:

"Son, those same men's fathers started holding those conferences forty years ago. Going to report something to the convention tonight? That is exactly what is the matter with this convention now, it's those conferences. If they had let the delegates confer instead of the leaders, why, your poor old father could have spent a life of usefulness instead of one listening to a man read off numbers, which we all knew better than he did.

"Son, if it's the Taggarts and Rockwells and Macks and Cramers and all of them that are conferring, you will die, like your poor old father, right at your post, listening for something to happen."

So please, Mr. Editor, take this story, and to-morrow, when I come home to dear old Dad, I will make him feel good. I won't tell him they are going to hold another conference.

ROPING A CRITIC

ROPING A CRITIC

PROLOGUE—These critics have been interviewing Actors (and us other people that appear on the stage) for years. And none of the interviews have ever been right, cause they never told the truth. Course they couldn't tell the truth about a lot of us, if they had he would have put us out of business. But they tried to be so kind to us and tell all the noble deeds that at the finish we had lost more friends than we had gained by the interview.

Now there is nothing interesting in an Actor but his act and you can get it at the box office price. This season you won't even have to form in line. If you can get a party of three to go with you you can get a rate.

But I figured there was something interesting about a Critic. Why, there are scientists that spend a life time studying a Toad.

Now, I might not find out as much as these Toad experts but I am going to look one of these Critics over at short range for about an hour—as Actors have got plenty of time—we are not bowing much nowadays.

So I picked out the Male of the Species as they are not as venomous as the females. I picked out Ashton Stevens, principally on account of him being frail of statue and because I had seen his name one time on an Ash Can for endorsing a Wintergarden Show.

Act I. DRESSING ROOM COLONIAL THEATER.—Enter Stevens made up as Critic. Gray suit, leather buttons, Black Felt Hat on upside down (same one Dick Little used to wear), middle finger of each hand calloused from knocking Actors. Smoking Pipe which is against all Theater rules, but on account of being critic managers can't say anything. The smoking really wasn't as bad as the Tobacco.

I started in to interview him and he started in like an Actor by lying. So I stopped him right there and said: "Say, this is not a theatrical interview. I am representing the Public and I want the real dope on Critics."

Q—Where were you born? Even a Critic has to be born.

A—I was born in San Francisco in 18—.

Q—Never mind when you were born—the reading public can tell by your jokes how old you are. Why were you born?

A—No answer.

Q—Well, if you can't think of a reason neither can I, so we will let that question go. Did Frisco ever find out that you were born there?

A—Yes.

Q—Is that why you left there?

A—No answer.

Q—When did you first show symptoms of becoming a Critic?

A—When I had lost my job at everything else.

Q—Didn't you tell your folks and didn't they have anything done for you to cure this?

A—I was afraid to tell them.

Q—Who gave you your first job Criticing?

A—William Randolph Hearst.

Q—Why did he give it to you?

A—He heard me play the Banjo.

Q—He heard you play the Banjo and gave you a job as a Critic. I suppose if he saw me throw a rope he would make me a Society Editor?

A—Oh, but it is not for my Banjoing that he keeps me now, its for my writings.

Q—Oh, he has forgot that you taught him to play the Banjo—that's why you still work for him?

A—No, its my writings. You see he took me from Frisco to New York and put me on the New York Journal.

Q—Now you say he took you there as Critic. Don't you really think he might have been getting a little rusty on the Banjo and needed it tuned?

A—No, I stayed there 4 years.

Q—What happened at the end of 4 years, did you all run out of Tunes, or did you break the Banjo or what?

A—No; then he promoted me to Chicago.

Q—You felt that you had taught him all you knew. Did you bring the Banjo out here with you?

A—Oh, yes I have it; I will bring it over now and show you how I play.

Q—Never mind bringing it over now or any other time. We will drop the Banjo until some time you feel you want a change of jobs. You can take it over to Medill McCormicks and teach him. He could at least amuse the other Senators with it and perhaps make you Editor of the Tribune. Now to get back to Criticing. What makes a Dramatic Critic?

A—Two Free Seats a Night on the Isle.

Q—Is it true that it is the only business in the World with absolutely no qualifications?

A—Yes; next to being a comedian with a Ziegfeld Show its the only thing that requires no training.

Q—Is it true that Dyspepsia is necessary to being a Critic?

A—Yes; its more prevalent now since the Movies come in.

Q—Don't you think that Prohibition has lowered the Standard of Dramatic Criticism?

A—Yes; among those that didn't look ahead and supply, I think that to be true.

Q—They still train on Scotch, don't they?

A—Well, they are not as well trained as they used to be.

Q—Don't you find a great many people that think they are Critics?

A—Yes, but I find very few that get paid for it.

Q—Do you believe in constructive Criticism?

A—No; I believe in entertaining Criticism.

Q—Do you get many letters kicking on your opinion?

A—Oh, yes; quite a few.

Q—In that way you can tell just how many read it, can't you? I read where three out of four of every newspaper started failed. What percentage of dramatic Criticisms do you think is responsible for this failure?

A—I don't know; I was never on a failing paper.

Q—That's pretty good; that's a Nifty. Now you Critics having never tried it, you don't realize just how hard it is to be an Actor?

A—Yes, the more plays we see the more we realize it.

Q—Now, you say you have worked for Mr. Hearst twenty-five years for teaching him the Banjo. What instrument did Brisbane teach him and do you think I could interest him in a Base Drum? I hammer a mean Blues on one of those things.

A—You might snare him with that. It takes two heads to make a drum.

Now, Dear Readers—both of you—if this little interview has made you feel more kindly toward the Dramatic Critics, and has brought their overworked profession to the high standards to which I have tried to honestly picture them, my work will not have been in vain.

"THE WORLD TOMORROW," AFTER THE MANNER OF GREAT JOURNALISTS.

"THE WORLD TOMORROW," AFTER THE MANNER OF GREAT JOURNALISTS.*

NOW for the last few months I have been writing and I have become ambitious and want to do "Bigger and Better things." I realize that my writings up to now have only appealed to the Morons. (That's not Mormon misspelled. It's *Morons,* just as it's spelled.) So I have been a close Student and admirer of some of our great editorial writers and I have tried to study their style and, beginning with this article, I am changing my entire method of Literature and I hereby bid Adieu to my Half-Wit Audience. (As a writer's Writings never appeal to a higher grade of intelligence than the Writer himself.) So, from now on, I am going to give these learned and heavy thinkers a run for their Laurels. I am out to make the front Page. My Column will be called The World Tomorrow, not only commenting on the news of Today but predicting what the morrow will bring forth.

* With apologies to Arthur Brisbane.

A Race Horse, In Memorandum, beats the great Zev, the International Favorite and My Own thrown in for good measure. That news will perhaps interest 40 million Human Beings, and 2,000 Bookmakers, while the news of the unearthing of a Prehistoric Skull at Santa Barbara, California, linking us up with the Neanderthal Age will only be appreciated by a small Majority of us thinking People. Some anthropologists, however, consider the extinct Neanderthal Man as a separate Species (Homo Neanderthalenis) intermediate between the Java Man (or Pithecanthropus). According to Linneaus, Humanity comprises four races: the Whites, having a light colored skin, belonging to the Caucasian race; the Blacks, the completest possible negation of White; the Republicans, form of genus Homo ape in his earliest Prehistoric State; and, last of the four Races the Democrat. The Democrat doubtless originated in the eastern Hemisphere. The main structural characters distinguishing him are his gait, the modification of the feet for walking instead of prehension, and the great Toe being nonopposable, and, most of all, the enormous development of the brain, and smooth rounded Skull.

But what cares the man of today for the Neanderthal Age! He is of the Speculative Age. If he can get 10 Dollars down on the Nose of a winner at about 15 to one, he don't care if we descend from Goat or Ape.

As Demosthenes, the Great William Jennings Bryan of his time, so aptly put it when he casually met Confucius, the originator of Mah-Jong on Epsom Downs: "Good Afternoon, countryman, art thee risking a few Shekels on thy favorite Crow Bait in this Race?" And Confucius pulled the following Nifty which has been handed down through the Ages, and made him the Philosopher or Shanghai:

"No, Demosthenes, Betting is a form of unintelligence. So long as we have betting, we will know we have the ignorant with us."

That little remark of Confucius was well said, and the fact that we had 40 million interested in the Race, and only a handful interested in the Neanderthal Man, proves we have a long way to go yet until Civilization is thoroughly reached.

The Crown Prince of Germany is to be allowed to return, proving that War don't pay. You only have to go back into History a short way to the Trojan

Wars. What happened to Priam the King of Troy when Prince Paris his Heir and Son was born? Eros, Goddess of Discord, threw out a Golden Apple to the most beautiful, and Juno, Minerva and Venus all claimed it. Paris was to decide. He gave the Apple to Venus. Helen of Troy, the most beautiful Woman in Sparta, got jealous of Paris and that culminated in the War of Troy. Troy was besieged for 9 years. This Trojan War alone should prove to the greedy Interests that War don't pay. And Sons born of Kings don't pay. A law should be passed that all offspring of Royal Birth should be of the feminine Gender.

An American army airman flies at the rate of 258 miles an hour. What does this astounding feat mean to the World? What did Napoleon say at Austerlitz in 1805, just after the battle of Ulm, and after the Old Corsican had rushed his troops from Cologne? He said, "An army travels on its Stomach."

Look at the progress that has been made in the mode of Transportation from the Napoleon days to this! I don't know exactly how far a man could travel in a day on his Stomach. If he had a good

Stomach and was an Apt Traveler he might make pretty good headway. There was no way in reckoning speed in those days as there was no way of fixing a speedometer on a Soldier's Stomach, but if you take a Soldier going away from the Enemy, and if his Stomach held out, he certainly ought to have had the abdominal record of his time

But has Congress heeded what the Airship is doing? No, they go ahead building Battleships which will be as useless as a shipping board. Transportation advances but our Lawmakers are still traveling on their Stomach.

Lloyd George goes home to England after inviting us to join in the Salvation of Europe. You have only to turn to Hugo's Oration on Voltaire to find out if we should meddle in the selfish affairs of European Turmoil. Hugo said: "Before going further, let us come to an understanding, Gentlemen, upon the word Abyss. There are good abysses: such are the abysses in which evil is engulfed. Rabelais warned royalty in Gargantua. Moliere warned the people at Tartuffe." That proves right there to any thinking person that we should not meddle in the affairs of these envious Nations. The more

Trouble you get them out of, the more they get into. No, the time has come when this Country has got to bank up our own fires for a cold morning. Just remember Cicero's words speaking at Glasgow in regard to America's participation in the World's War: "La premiere femme du monde la tete montee en se couchant." Those who want to adjust Europe's Carburetor should remember Horace Greeley's immortal Gag: "Go west, young man, *Not* east."

A Lady in Chicago is arrested for killing a casual acquaintance. That's news. If she had killed her Husband or Lover that would be commonplace. But friends are seldom killed. What does the 8th chapter, second verse, of the first Book of Matthew teach us? That verse should be enough to teach us that friendship should be trusted. We will never have true civilization until we have learned to recognize the rights of others.

Judge Gary, the head of the great Steel Corporation, eats only the white of a soft boiled egg for breakfast. Which should be a lesson to some of you who think you have to eat the whole egg to subsist. We should look and learn from our Men who have Done Things. Read Einstein's Theory on what constitutes over-gorging. He says: "Light rays, if obstructed, have an observed constant velocity irrespective of the relative velocity between the observer." That should show even the ignorant when they have enough.

A little Girl in Brooklyn started to school and forgot her books and had to go home for them. There you have a bit of news that is valuable. We are at that age when we are rushing headlong and paying no attention to small details. It's only the big things of life that interest us. For instance, the little Girl was only interested in getting to the School, not in what she had when she got there. If we only stopped to realize that it is really after all the little things that count, why, we would be a wiser and more contented race. People that can't remember should remember what Socrates said to Plato on the subject of forgetfulness. He said: "Where then I wonder shall we find Justice and Injustice in it? With which have we contemplated? Has it simultaneously made its entrance?"

A Professor of Columbia University won a prize by writing a Book in 15 hours. That's a good thing. The quicker the Authors write them the quicker they can get to some useful work. But if Pascal were on earth today and heard of that feat he would say: "That's fine, Professor, but what did you do with the other 10 Hours?"

It takes two and a half Tons of Marks to buy a Stein of Beer in Berlin. Before the War you could have bought two and a half Tons of Beer for a Mark. What does Wall Street think of that? It shows you that selfish Interests can't rule the People, when they make up their mind to rebel.

P.S. You see I have an Encyclopedia, too.

SETTLING THE AFFAIRS OF THE WORLD IN MY OWN WAY

"IF THEY HAVEN'T GOT ENOUGH WATER IN THERE TO FILL THE HARBOR, WE WILL HAVE TO ASK THE NEIGHBORS TO DRAIN THEIR CORN LIQUOR."

SETTLING THE AFFAIRS OF THE WORLD IN MY OWN WAY

WELL, they brought our Soldiers back from Germany. Would have brought them back sooner but we didn't have anybody in Washington who knew where they were. We had to leave 'em over there so they could get the Mail that was sent to them during the war. Had to leave 'em over there anyway; two of them hadn't married yet.

Since I wrote you last, an awful lot has happened at the Studio in Washington, D. C. You know out where they make the Movies, the place we make them is called the Studio. We are a great deal alike in lots of respects. We make what we think will be two kinds of Pictures, Comedy and Drama, or sad ones. Now you take the Capitol at Washington, that's the biggest Studio in the World. We call ours, Pictures, when they are turned out. They call theirs Laws, or Bills. It's all the same thing. We often make what we think is Drama, but when it is shown it is received by the audience as Comedy. So the uncertainty is about equal both places.

The way to judge a good Comedy is by how long it will last and have people talk about it. Now Congress has turned out some that have lived for years and people are still laughing about them, and as for Sad productions, they have turned out some that for sadness make "Over the Hills" look like a roaring farce.

Girls win a little State Popularity Contest that is conducted by some Newspaper; then they are put into the Movies to entertain 110 million people who they never saw or know anything about. Now that's the same way with the Capitol Comedy Company of Washington. They win a State Popularity Contest backed by a Newspaper and are sent to Washington to turn out Laws for 110 million people they never saw.

They have what they call Congress, or the Lower House. That compares to what we call the Scenario Department. That's where somebody gets the idea of what he thinks will make a good Comedy Bill or Law, and they argue around and put it into shape.

Then it is passed along, printed, or shot, or Photographed, as we call it; then it reaches the Senate or the Cutting and Titling Department. Now, in our Movie Studios we have what we call Gag Men whose sole business is to just furnish some little Gag, or Amendment as they call it, which will get a laugh or perhaps change the whole thing around.

Now the Senate has what is considered the best and highest priced Gag Men that can be collected anywhere. Why, they put in so many little gags or amendments that the poor Author of the thing don't know his own story.

They consider if a man can sit there in the Studio in Washington and just put in one funny amendment in each Bill, or production, that will change it from what it originally meant, why, he is considered to have earned his pay. Take for Instance the Prohibition Production that was introduced in the Congress or Scenario Department as a Comedy.

Well, when it came up in the Senate, one of the Gag or Title Men says, "I got an Idea; instead of this just being a joke, and doing away with the Saloons and Bar Rooms, why I will put in a Title here that will do away with everything." So they sent around to all the Bars in Washington and got a Quorum and released what was to be a harmless little Comedy—made over into a Tragedy.

Then they put out a Production called the Non-Taxable Bond, or "Let the Little Fellow Pay." Well it had a certain Vogue for a while with the Rich. But it flopped terribly in the cheaper priced Houses.

Another one they put out a lot of you will remember was called the Income or Sur-Tax. It was released under the Title of, "Inherit your money and your Sur-Tax is Lighter."

The main Character in this one was a working man on salary, with no Capital investment to fall back on, paying more on his income than the fellow who has his original Capital and draws his money just from interest. That Production has been hissed in some of the best houses.

They started to put on a Big one that everybody in America was looking forward to and wanted them to produce called, "The Birth Of the Bonus," or "How Could You Forget so Soon!" But on account of Finances they couldn't produce that and the "Non-Taxable Bond Production" both, so they let the Bonus one go.

They have been working on two dandies. One

is called, "Refund, Refund, I am always refunding You." It's principally for British Trade.

Then they got a Dandy Comedy; well, it's really a serial as they put it on every year. Everybody in the whole Studio is interested in it and get a share of it. It's really their yearly Bonus in addition to their Salary. It's called, "Rivers and Harbors," or, "I'LL GET MINE."

They got some of the funniest Scenes in there where they take 56 million Dollars of the People's money and they promise to make a lot of Streams wide enough to fish in. Now I saw a Pre-Release of it and here are some of the Real Titles. In Virginia, their Gag Senator has thought of a River called the MATTIPONI. In North Carolina, their Title writer, Overman, thought of a name, the CONTENTNEA CREEK. But the funniest Title in the whole Production is the CALOOSEHATCHIE, in Florida. It's located right in the fairway of a Golf Course and Congress must move it or in two years it will be filled up with Golf Balls.

Then they have a scene applying for funds to dredge TOMBIGBEE CREEK, and the BIG SUNFLOWER, in Mississippi. Well, that's money well spent to do that, as they may find some of the missing population.

And there's the CLATSKANIE in Oregon. Now what I am wondering is how our Navy is to make the Jump from the Harbor of Tombigbee to the Docks in Oregon on the Clatskanie. Of course, that's a different appropriation or production, and will be arranged later.

Now I am off my Senators from Oklahoma, especially Robert Owen, who is a part Cherokee Indian like myself (and as proud of it as I am). Now I got names right there on my farm where I was born that are funny, too, and Owen don't do a thing to get me a Harbor on the VERDIGRIS river at OOLAGAH in what used to be the District of COOWEESCOOWEE (before we spoiled the best Territory in the World to make a State).

Right across the river from me lives JIM TICK-EATER. Now suppose a foreign fleet should come up there. We can't ask those Turtles and Water Moccasins to move out without Government sanction. If they haven't got enough water in there to fill the harbor (we are only 18 miles from NOWATER, Oklahoma), why, we will have to ask all the Neighbors to drain their Corn Liquor from their stills in there for a couple of days. Then we could float the Leviathan.

Of course I don't get anything done for my Harbor because my River really *exists*.

Now, Folks, why patronise California-made Productions? The Capitol Comedy Co. of Washington, D. C., have never had a failure. They are every one, 100 percent funny, or 100 percent Sad.

They are making some changes in their cast down there and later I will tell you about that. Also something about the Director.

So long, Folks, I will meet you at the Naval Manœuvers on CONTENTNEA CREEK next year.

A SKINNY DAKOTA KID WHO MADE GOOD

A SKINNY DAKOTA KID WHO MADE GOOD

OUT of the west came a little skinny runt kid, born out in the hills of South Dakota. On Sundays the Cowpunchers and Ranchers would meet and have Cow Pony races. On account of his being small he was lifted up and a surcingle was strapped around over his legs and around the horse. He was taken to the starting line on a straightaway and was "lapped and tapped" off. He had the nerve and he seemed to have the head. So they cut the surcingle and he got so he could sit up there on one of those postage stamp things they call a Jockey's saddle. He kept riding around these little Country Shooting Gallery meets, and Merry-Go-Round Gatherings, until he finally got good enough to go to a real race track at New Orleans. There he saw more Horses in one race than he had ever seen at one track before.

His first race he ran 2nd. Then he said to himself, "Why run second? Why not run first?" And he did. They began to notice that this kid really *savied* a Horse. He spoke their language. Horses seemed to know when the kid was up. He carried a Bat (Jockey's term for a whip) but he never seemed to use it. Other Jocks would come down the stretch whipping a Horse out when the best he could finish would be 4th or 5th. But not this kid. When he couldn't get in the money he never punished them. He hand rode them. He could get more out of a Horse with his hands than another Jock could get with the old Battery up both sleeves.

He got to be recognized as one of the best, and he passed from one Stable to another until he landed with the biggest, a real Trainer and a Real Sportsman-Owner. How many thousands of People in every line come to New York every year that want to make good, get ahead and be recognized! They come by the millions. How many, if anything happened to them, would get even a passing Notice in the busy and overcrowded New York Press. If some Millionaire died, the best he could get would be a column. Then perhaps it wouldn't be read through by a dozen. But what blazoned across the front pages of every Metropolitan daily a few days ago, in bigger headlines than a Presidential Nomination, bigger than the Prince of Wales will get on his arrival? In a race at Saratoga Springs, N. Y., a Horse had fallen and carried down with him a little skinny Kid (that had slept in his youth not in a 5th Avenue Mansion but in Box Stalls all over the Country with Horses, the Horses he knew how to ride and the Horses that loved to run their best for him).

Here was the Headline: "SANDE IS HURT. He may never ride again." They don't have to give even his first name; few know it. They don't have to explain who he is. They don't have to tell which Rockefeller or Morgan it was. It was just Sande. There is only one. Our Sande! The boy who had carried America's colors to Victory over England's great Papyrus and their Premier Jockey Steve Donohue.

The Ambulance rushes on the track and picks him up; it is followed by hundreds afoot, running. The entire grand stands of people rush to the temporary Track Hospital to see how Sande is, and hoping and praying that it's not serious. He revives long enough to tell his Wife he is all right. Game kid that. Then he faints again. Mrs. Vanderbilt and the elite of Society are assisting and doing all they can to help. A personal Physician to a President of the United States is working over him. He could not have shown any more anxiety over the President than he did over this kid. When the thousands of pleasure seekers and excitement hunters rushed from the stands and saw them lifting that frail lifeless looking form from the track Ambulance there was not one that wouldn't have given an Arm off their body if they had thought it would save his Life, and that goes for Touts, and Grooms, and Swipes, as well as the Public.

Some western people who don't know are always saying Easterners have no Heart, everything is for themselves and the Dough. Say, don't tell me that! Geography don't change Human Nature. If you are Right, people are for you whether it's in Africa or Siberia. A wire was sent by Mr. Widener, a millionaire Racing Official, to Dr. Russell the great Specialist of Roosevelt Hospital, New York, "Come at once. Spare no expense. SANDE is Hurt!" That's all Secretary Slemp could do if President Coolidge was hurt.

Mr. Sinclair withdrew all Horses from the remaining Races. He would withdraw them for Life if he knew it would restore this Kid who worked for him, back to normal again.

Now what made this One Hundred and Ten Pounds (half portion of physical manhood) beloved by not only the racing Public but by the masses who never bet a cent on a Horse race in their lives? The same thing that will make a man great in any line—his absolute HONESTY. The racing public are very fickle and when they lose they are apt to lay blame on almost any quarter. But win or lose, they knew it was not Sande. To have insinuated to one of them that he ever pulled a Horse, would have been taking your Life in your hands. What do you suppose he could have gotten out of some bunch of betting Crooks to have pulled Zev in the big International Race? Why, enough to retire on and never have to take another chance with his Life by riding. He could have done it on the back stretch and no one would have ever known.

Ability is all right but if it is not backed up by Honesty and Public confidence you will never be a Sande. A man that don't love a Horse, there is something the matter with him. If he has no sympathy for the man that does love Horses then there is something worse the matter with him. The best a Man can do is to arrive at the top of his chosen profession. I have always maintained that one Profession is deserving of as much honor as another provided it is honorable.

Through some unknown process of reasoning we have certain things that are called Arts, and to be connected with them raises you above your fellow Man. Say, how do they get that way? If a Man happens to take up Painting and becomes only a mediocre painter, why should he be classed above the Bricklayer who has excelled every other Bricklayer? The Bricklayer is a true Artist in his line or he could not have reached the top. The Painter has not been acclaimed the best in his line hence the Bricklayer is superior. Competition is just as keen in either line. In fact there are more good bricklayers than Painters. If you are the best Taxi Driver you are as much an Artist as Kreisler. You save lives by your skilful driving. That's a meritorious profession, is it not?

A Writer calls himself a Literary Man or an Artist. There are thousands of them, and all, simply because they write, are termed Artists. Is there a Sande among them? Caruso was great, but he had only to show ability. He didn't have to demonstrate any honesty. Nobody tried to keep him from singing his best by bribery.

Now if you think the Racing Public and millions of well wishers are hoping for this Kid's recovery, what about the Horses? They knew him better than the Humans did. Why, that Horse would have broke his own neck rather than hurt Sande. Who is going to ride him in the next race and make him win and not whip him?—not Sande. Who is going to sit on him just where he will be the easiest to carry? Not Sande. Who is going to lean over and whisper in his ear and tell him when to go his best? Not Sande. Who is going to carry a Bat and not use it? Not Sande. Who is going to watch the hand on that starting Barrier and have him headed the right way just when the starter springs it? Not Sande. No, the Horses are the ones who are going to miss him.

If we could speak their language like he can, here are a few conversations that you will hear through the cracks in the Box Stalls: "Gee, I can't run; I don't seem to get any help. I wish Sande were back."

A three year old replies, "I wish there was something we could do. If they would just let us go up to the Hospital and talk to him he would savy," "I wish we had him here in a Box Stall. I would stand up the rest of my life and give him my bed. I would fix him some Clean Hay to lay on. He don't want those White Caps and Aprons running around. He wants to lay on a Horse Blanket, and have his busted Leg wrapped up with Bandages like he knows how to use on ours. I bet they ain't even got Absorbine up there. That Kid would rather have a Bran Mash than all that Goo they will feed him with up there."

The Old Stake Horse 4 stalls down the line overhears and replies: "Sure, I bet they have one of them Bone Specialists. What that Kid needs is a good Vet."

The old Selling Plater butts in: "Sure, we could cheer him up if he was here. Them Foreigners up there don't speak his Tongue. That kid is part Horse. Remember how he used to kid wid us when he would be working us out at daylight when the rest of the Star Jocks was in feathers. One morning I told him if he didn't quit waking me up so early in the morning I was going to buck him off. He got right back at me; he said, 'If you do I will get you left at the Post your next race.' Gee, he sure did throw a scare into me. And, say, you couldn't loaf on that Bird either. He knew when you was loafing and when you was trying. I throwed up my tail one hot day to make him think I was all through. He give me one cut with the Bat and I dropped that tail and left there so fast I could have run over Man of War. Gee, those were great days; Do youse reckon Zev knows anything about it? I hope they don't tell him; it would break his heart. He sure did love that kid."

Patient readers, Lincoln went down in History as "HONEST Abe," BUT HE NEVER WAS A JOCKEY. If he had been a Jockey he might have gone down as just "Abe."

TAKING THE CURE, BY THE SHORES OF CAT CREEK

"IF YOU DON'T GET WELL AND THROW AWAY YOUR CRUTCHES I GET NOTHING OUT OF IT."

TAKING THE CURE, BY THE SHORES OF CAT CREEK

NOW, in my more or less checkered career before the more or less checkered Public, I have been asked to publicly indorse everything from Chewing Gum, Face Beautifiers, Patent Cocktail Shakers, Ma Junk Sets, even Corsets, Cigarettes, and Chewing Tobacco, all of which I didn't use or know anything about. But I always refused.

You never heard me boosting for anything, for I never saw anything made that the fellow across the street didn't make something just as good.

But, at last, I have found something that I absolutely know no one else has something just as good as, for an all-seeing Nature put this where it is and it's the only one he had, and by a coincidence it is located in the Town near the ranch where I was born and raised.

So I hereby and hereon come out unequivocally (I think that's the way you spell it) in favor of a place that has the water that I *know* will cure you. You might ask, cure me of what? Why, cure you of anything—just name your disease and dive in.

Claremore, Oklahoma, is the birthplace of this Aladdin of health waters. Some misguided Soul named it RADIUM WATER, but Radium will never see the day that it is worth mentioning in the same breath as this Magic Water. Why, to the afflicted and to all suffering Humanity, a Jug of this Water is worth a wheelbarrow full of Radium. Still, even under the handicap of a cheap name, this liquid Godsend has really cured thousands.

Now you may say, "Oh you boost it because you live there," but I don't want you to think so little of me that you would think I would misguide a sick person, just for the monetary gain to my Home Town. We don't need you that bad. The city is on a self supporting basis without Patients, just by shipping the Water to Hot Springs, Ark., Hot Springs, Va., West Baden, Ind., and Saratoga, N. Y.

Now, as to a few of the Ignorant who might still be in the dark as to where the Home of this Fountain of Youth is located, I will tell you. I shouldn't waste my time on such Low Brows, but unfortunately they get sick and need assistance the same as the 95 Million others who already know where Claremore is located.

It is located, this Mecca of the ill, about 17 hundred miles west of New York, (either City or State, depends on which ever one you happen to be in). You bear a little south of west, after leaving New York, till you reach Sol McClellan's place, which is just on the outskirts of Claremore. Before you get into the City proper, if you remember about 500 miles back, you passed another Town. Well, that was St. Louis, most of which is in Illinois.

Now, if you are in the North, and happen to get something the matter with you, we are 847 and a half miles South by West from Gary, Indiana. We have cured hundreds of people from Chicago, Ill. from Gun shot wounds inflicted in attempted murders and robberies. There is only one way to avoid being robbed of anything in Chicago and that is not to have anything.

If you are from Minneapolis, our Radium Water guarantees to cure you of everything but your Swedish accent. If you are from St. Paul, we can cure you of everything but your ingrown hatred for Minneapolis.

I will admit that these waters have quite a peculiar odor as they have a proportion of Sulphur and other unknown ingredients, but visitors from

Kansas City, who are used to a Stock Yard breeze, take this wonderful water home as a Perfume.

Approaching this City from the North, don't get it confused with Oolagah, Oklahoma, my original Birthplace, which is 12 miles to the north, as both towns have Post Offices.

From the west, if you are afflicted and you are sure to be or you wouldn't have gone out there, why Claremore is just 1900 miles due east of Mojarve, California, one of the few Towns which Los Angeles has not voted into their Cafeteria. You come east till you reach an Oil Station at a road crossing. This oil station is run by a man named St. Clair. You will see a lot of men pitching Horseshoes. Well, that is the Post Office of Tulsa, Oklahoma, and the men are Millionaires pitching Horseshoes for Oil Wells or for each other's wives.

You should, by this description, have the place pretty well located in your minds. Now, if you are living in the South and are afflicted with a Cotton Crop under a Republican Administration, or with the Klu Klux, or with the Hook Worm, we guarantee to rid you of either or all of these in a course of 24 Baths.

Claremore is located just 905 miles north of Senator Pat Harrison's Mint Bed in Mississippi. In coming from the Gulf Country some have got off the road and had to pass through Dallas, Texas, but have found out their mistake and got back on the main road at Ft. Worth before losing all they had. You easily can tell Ft. Worth. A fellow will be standing down in front of the Drug Store making a speech.

Now, before reaching Claremore, you will pass, even though it's in the middle of the day, a place where you think it's night and you won't know what is the matter. Well, that's Muskogee, Oklahoma, and this darkness is caused by the Color scheme of the population, so put on your headlights and go on in. This Muskogee is really a parking space for cars entering Claremore. Of course, if you want to drive on into the Town of Claremore proper, its only 60 miles through the suburbs from here.

The City is located on Cat Creek, and instead of having a lot of Streets like most Towns and Cities, we have combined on one street. In that way no Street is overlooked.

You might wonder how we discovered this Blarney Stone of Waters. In the early days, us old timers there, always considered these Wells more as an Odor than as a Cure. But one day a man come in there who had been raised in Kansas and he had heard in a roundabout way of people bathing, although he had never taken one. So, by mistake, he got into this Radium Water.

He was a one armed man—he had lost an Arm in a rush to get into a Chautauqua Tent in Kansas to hear Bryan speak on Man Vs. Monkey. Well he tried this Bath and it didn't kill him and he noticed that he was beginning to sprout a new arm where he had lost the old one, so he kept on with the Baths and it's to him that we owe the discovery of this wonderful curative Water. Also he was the Pioneer of Bathers of Kansas, as now they tell me it's no uncommon thing to have a Tub in most of their larger towns.

Now, it has been discovered that you can carry a thing too far and overdo it, so we don't want you there too long. A man come there once entirely Legless and stayed a week too long and went away a Centipede.

I want to offer here my personal Testimonial of what it did to me. You see, after this Kansas Guy started it, why, us old Timers moved our bathing from the River into a Tub. Now, at that time, I was practically Tongue tied and couldn't speak out in private much less in Public. Well, after 12 baths, I was able to go to New York and make after dinner speeches. I stopped in Washington on the way and saw how our Government was run and that gave me something funny to speak about.

So, in thanking the Water, I also want to thank the Government for making the whole thing possible. Now, had I taken 24 baths I would have been a Politician, so you see I stopped just in time.

The only thing I get out of this is I have the "Thrown Away Crutch Privilege." If you don't get well and throw away your Invalid Chair or crutches I get nothing out of it, so that is why we give you a square deal. If you are not cured, I don't get your Crutches. There is no other resort in the World that works on that small a margin.

W. J. Bryan drank one drink of this Water and turned against Liquor. Senator La Follette drank two drinks of it and turned against everything. So remember Claremore, The Carlsbad of America, where the 'Frisco Railroad crosses the Iron Mountain Railroad, not often, but every few days.

THE END